Concept and Text
**Roving Writers**

Photographer
**Karam Puri**
Additional Photographs
**Akshay Mahajan**
**Vipul Sangoi**

Designer
**Vipul Sangoi, Raindesign**

Project Management
**Roving Writers,**
**a unit of SAITA Consulting Pvt. Ltd.**

**©Trio Omni Media, 2008**
Trio Omni Media
Vipul Plaza, Sun City, Sector -54
Gurgaon -122002, India
Tel: + 91.124.4353600

ISBN 978-81-906831-0-4
First Edition, 2008

Printed by
Nutech Photolithographers, New Delhi, India

**Additional Photo Credit**
**Akshay Mahajan**: 2, 21, 28 (bottom), 30, 31, 50 (bottom), 52, 55, 62
(bottom), 65, 70, 71, 72, 73, 74, 75, 76, 77, 81, 92, 93, 94, 96, 98 (top),
99 (top), 102 (top), 104, 105, 109, 110 (bottom right), 112, 114, 117,
125, 128, 132, 137, 140, 147 (top), 148, 153 (bottom), 154, 155, 156,
157, 172, 222, 222, 244, 245 (bottom)
**Vipul Sangoi**: 148, 149, 152 (top), 165
**Fotomedia**: 124
**Hyphen Films**: 136

# Gujarat
## a journey....

GJ.1.AV. 700

# Contents

My grandfather was a man of little words. Which is why I found it ironic that this dedication should require any. But we must stick to certain norms now, mustn't we? He would have liked this description of himself, but far more importantly, he would have adored what is to follow. The images. Not just any images; images of his beloved Gujarat. I want to call them 'vibrant' and 'colourful', but somehow the words seem too clichéd.

Over the years my family has searched for a book that did justice to the state, and somehow, apart from a few odd exceptions, we merely found book upon book that displayed one side of Gujarat - aridity. What of her diverse ethnicity? Her architecture? Her animals and crafts? Upon failing to find what we were looking for, we decided to create it ourselves. This was a project rife with glitches and hiccups, and it spread itself messily over three long years. The second year being particularly hard because Dada decided to leave us.

The gentlest of men with the kindest of souls, Dada's departure quietened us all, and in turn the project. Something people don't know about my grandfather is that when he wanted something, he could be stubborn in an almost childish way, perseveringly demanding his desire. After a while, something strange happened. The book seemed to take on his characteristics. Sitting patiently waiting to be completed, it gnawed at one. "And what about me?" it asked silently.

What you're holding is a labour of love. This is for Dada, finally, and I'm pretty certain he would have been pleased.

Karuna Ezara Parikh
New Delhi, August 2008

# Introduction

**If you looked** at India's shape the way it had often been represented through calendar art in the last century, as a woman in a saree with long flowing hair, or as Bharat Mata, a Mother Goddess whose soul represents our nation, then Gujarat would be her right hand. In this picture, it will be a crooked hand, perhaps held up in benediction and held close to the body, unlike the other one extended gracefully to the left. The bony elbow would be Kutch but the arm will be rounded, even a little plump.

It is a fanciful image, but it is an image that will speak to the average Gujarati, for the average Gujarati is big on stories and colour, myth and construct. These are a myriad people: where men wear large silver ear-studs, sleeveless vests and multi-coloured turbans, and women wear solid blacks with unfussy veils. These are also men who wear polyester pants and bend over delicate machinery, trying to slice a diamond just right. And, these are women who can run a lot of things – from the local fiefdom at a sea port to a snacks business worth millions of rupees. These are people who like to venerate and have venerated a freedom fighter such as **Mohandas Karamchand Gandhi** as a saint, a 'mahatma', and as a father, 'Bapu'.

These are people who have fought hard for what they cherished – their right to make a living off their land, their right to their rivers and forests, their right to justice. These are also a people who have not always stayed put. They have arrived – and continue to arrive – from other parts of the country and they have also sailed forth into new continents, in search of a better life.

Understanding Gujarat is no easy task. Like much of India, it is a complex state that has resisted homogeneity for centuries past. Intimate histories, conventions, clothes, crafts, beliefs, affiliations – all of these change from district to district.

What is now a state that we call Gujarat was the western wing of a vast empire spanning half the body of the subcontinent under powerful emperors like Chandragupta Maurya, Ashoka and Akbar. Then, it was split into many hundreds of large kingdoms and tiny princely estates, most of them controlled by the British when India became a 'colony'. In 1947, the land was split into India and Pakistan and what remained on the Indian side of the border was a part of a larger state, the Bombay Presidency. It was only in 1960 that a separate state called Gujarat was carved out on the basis of language. An overwhelming majority of people living within its borders, irrespective of religion or caste, speak Gujarati, although there are several tribes with their own distinct languages and several million who consider Kutchi their native tongue.

There is Pakistan to the west and the Indian states of Madhya Pradesh to the east, Rajasthan to the north, Maharashtra (and the union territories of Daman and Diu) to the south and the sea all round from the west to the south. It is also the state with the longest coastline and, not surprisingly, has a long, enriching history of maritime trade and cultural openness resulting from the constant contact with diverse races and community practices. As evidenced by the excavated remains of the Indus Valley Civilisation in the region, commercial, artistic and cultural exchanges have been part of people's lives for over four thousand years.

Gujarat is one of the most urbanised and industrialised states in the country. It is also known to be a 'rich' state, in that its average per capita income is nearly twenty percent higher than the national

Title inset
*Within the mosque at Junagadh Fort*

Top
*Dalpat Ram (1820 - 1898), at the forefront of modern Gujarati literature; an essayist and dramatist whose masterpiece Venacharitra is one of the keenest displays of literary humour and wit*

Left
*Elders, Ahmedabad*

average, although differences between the haves and have-nots remain wide enough to be noticeable. The state contributes nearly twenty percent of the industrial output in India. Many of the large industrial conglomerates are in sectors such as petrochemicals, pharmaceuticals and textiles. However, there are thousands of smaller businesses whose interests range from the homely vegetable oils to electric engineering and cement. Gujarat is also known for its near-monopoly on the international diamond cutting-and-polishing business and for being home to the world's largest ship-breaking yard, in Alang.

There are a few stereotypes about the 'typical' Gujarati – such as a strong entrepreneurial streak, a head for business, a sweet tooth, a tendency to favour compromise over conflict, a feet-on-the-ground approach to life and a love of laughter – and, like with all stereotypes, there is some truth buried in there.

The average Gujarati's love of laughter might be the trait that drives the production and staging of dozens of plays each year, most of which are comedies constructed around families or marriages.

It is also true, for instance, that many of the Gujaratis living in Mumbai were traders, big or small; some owned the local grocery shops while others dabbled in the stock market, but it is also true that a greater number simply worked in mills or on farms. The cowherd, the nomadic camel-breeder, the cotton-grower, the ghazal-spinning poet, the sociologist, the linguist, the fashion designer, the political activist is as much Gujarati as the enterprising youngster with a smart plan to make pots of money.

The success stories that have passed into the folklore of commerce include Dhirubhai Ambani, who set out with only a few thousand rupees in his pockets but died one of India's, indeed the world's, richest men. Another story is that of the milkmen and milkmaids from Anand who formed a dairy co-operative: Amul, which is one of India's best-known brands and one of the largest dairy producers in the world. Equally significant is the fact that the state has a long history of protest, organised workforces and activism, right from the ancient era down to the independence struggle.

Post-independence, there has been considerable investment in education. These investments have been far-reaching and wide-ranging. There are high-profile institutes for management, design and technology, where many young students would give an arm and a leg to get accepted. There is MS University in Vadodara, which has a history of encouraging research and a fine arts tradition that gave the nation some of its best artists.

Gujarat was built on the foundations of a composite culture and even today, learning about its traditions is akin to tracing variations on a broad theme; in fact, there are so many variations that it may be hard to isolate and identify each one. It is rumoured that there are more than three thousand festivals in the state if one takes into account all the tribes, communities and myriad shades of faith and ritual, ranging from kite-flying to intoxicated dancing, from painted faces to whirling, drum-beating men, and lighting clay lamps to burning sandalwood at a fire temple.

Ultimately, to seek out the soul of any place, one must seek out its people. And, it is not enough to look at them, take their pictures and draw them into conversation. At the heart of the process of discovery lies an attempt to open one's own soul to them: to delve into their broad political history and then to also stand at their side and listen while they go about creating a very small, intimate history that nobody will remember, perhaps. One must wander about the busiest, most unwelcoming alleys and allow oneself to be drawn into a bargain. One must stand in a corner of a cemetery or watch a mother plead for the pleasure of a baby.

In a simple, unpretentious way, that is what this book has attempted. For you may hear about, read about, look at and still fail to comprehend the soul of a place unless you are willing to stand under a bright sun, open your eyes really wide and see the truths that are so plain that they appear unremarkable.

Top
*Entrance archway into the Swaminarayan Mandir made entirely of wood, Ahmedabad*

Left
*The Great Mosque at Champaner, 15c.; a UNESCO World Heritage Site. In the background you can spot the hills which house the Pavagarh fort and temple complex with a lake on top*

Left
*Swaminarayan Mandir, Ahmedabad; a
live and colourful testament to faith*

Top
*Angelic carvings in a church in
the old city of Ahmedabad*

He gave to the world a new kind of philosophy. That of the ineluctable dignity of man, of every man, whether ruled or ruling, free or enslaved, whether white, black, brown or yellow. He called it truth and non-violence. He called it patriotism. He called it religion.

# The Ineluctable Dignity of Man

## Mahatma Gandhi. Gandhiji. Bapu.

### The great soul. Universally respected. The father of the nation.

In Mohandas Karamchand Gandhi, Gujarat found the best of its traditions merging. A natural pragmatism that may have been rooted in his business-family upbringing; a refusal to put up with injustice and oppression; an unshakable secularism that may have come to him through his mother's faith... What emerged was the reed-thin, old man who leaned on a stick, fasted, spun rough khadi and stood at the helm of a nation's march towards independence.

Born on October 2, 1869, Gandhi came from a well-off family. His father, Karamchand, was the diwan of Porbandar, which was one of the three hundred-odd princely states in the region at the time. At eighteen, he set sail for England to study law. Before leaving, he had promised his mother that he would not touch wine, women or meat, during his stint abroad. Hard promises to keep in western society, then or now. After a brief foray into 'society', which involved dressing in the best suits and going to dance-halls, the young man turned back to his simple ways; he also learned to treat his vegetarianism with conviction rather than awkwardness, even writing articles and forming clubs centered on vegetarianism.

In 1891, he passed the Bar exam and went back to India, only to find that his mother was already dead. What followed was a period of personal struggle; he knew little about the laws governing India and it was hard to find work in Rajkot or Bombay. When he did find his first case, he could not say a single word in the court. He ended up returning the fee to his client and, naturally, sank into a deep despair.

He returned to Rajkot and started a low-key career drafting petitions until he got an offer to deal with a civil suit in South Africa. He went to Durban in 1893, where a lifetime of protest was initiated, starting with a refusal to take off his turban in court. The well-known incident of the train happened on a journey from Durban to Pretoria. He had a first-class ticket but was not allowed to travel in the first-class compartment, quite simply because he was not white. Until then, he hadn't experienced the worst of imperial racism and the ugly discrimination against coloured people. Smarting as he was, he decided to stick it out. Not to escape back to the relative comfort of India, but to stay and fight.

He appealed to conscience, he pleaded in print, he argued in courts, he protested on the streets. But, he did not raise his hand to hurt another person. At the same time, he began to mobilise the disenfranchised Indian immigrant community in South Africa, a minority that was governed by crushing economic and social laws. After fourteen years, when he had failed to prevent legislation that would prove unjust to the Asian minority, he decided to try a new strategy – passive resistance, which he called 'Satyagraha'. As a result, he was arrested for the first time and when he was released, he was badly beaten up by fellow-Indians who had suspected him of being a 'traitor' to the Indian cause! After the second arrest and as news of his methods of protest spread to India and England, both Delhi and London began to pressurise South Africa to negotiate with Gandhi. Eventually, many of the Indian demands were conceded.

### Mohandas Karamchand Gandhi

1869 : Born, October 2

1891 : Passed Bar Exam

1893 : Went to Durban

1907 : New strategy - Satyagraha

1908 : First arrest

1915 : Return to India

1919 : Launched Satyagraha in India

1930 : Dandi March

1942 : Quit India Movement

1947 : Indian Independence

1948 : Shot by Nathuram Godse, January 30

'I DO NOT WANT MY HOUSE TO BE WALLED IN ON ALL SIDES AND MY WINDOWS TO BE STUFFED. I WANT THE CULTURES OF ALL LANDS TO BE BLOWN ABOUT MY HOUSE AS FREELY AS POSSIBLE. BUT I REFUSE TO BE BLOWN OFF MY FEET BY ANY.'

— MAHATMA GANDHI.

Title inset
*Sabarmati Ashram; The original charka Gandhiji used, housed in a glass case*

Top 1
*Bapu's spectacles*

Top 2
*Words that influenced a nation. Plaque on a wall at Sabarmati Ashram*

Right
*Sabarmati Ashram; Gandhiji's room - simplicity and action, symbolic of the man*

Page 10-11
*Shahibaug Area, Ahmedabad; tiled mural of Gandhiji*

The **truth**.
The **truth** runs about on a bicycle in a shocking pink turban and a dhoti and a shepherd's stick, after three donkeys, each of them with one left foreleg tied to the hind-leg and a black thread around their knees.
The **truth** is embedded on a wall of mosaic tiled 'Gandhi Bhajan'
The **truth** is a camel's lower lip, chewing breakfast on his way to work on Monday morning.

मेरा जीवन ही मेरा संदेश है।

મારું જીવન એ જ મારો સંદેશ

My life

is my message.

MKGandhi

After about two decades, Gandhi returned home in 1915, having gone from being a lawyer to a resolute political leader. India and its budding nationalist movement had heard of MK Gandhi and the leaders received him with open arms. Yet, for a year, he was not to express a single opinion in public. This was supposed to be a period of probation imposed by his mentor, **GK Gokhale**.

Gandhi knew a lot about struggle, but not enough about the political environment in India; so he travelled and watched and listened. In the meantime, he set up an ashram, first at Kochrab and then in Ahmedabad, on the banks of the Sabarmati.

From 1919 onwards, he launched Satyagraha in India. Non-violent non-cooperation was his chief weapon. Boycotts, strikes, marches and millions courting arrest: these were the forces he used. At the same time, Gandhi became Gandhiji, the mahatma. His austere lifestyle and deep religiosity had struck a chord with the masses and they embraced him as a saint as much as a political leader.

When he was arrested, the non-cooperation movement floundered even as communal violence flared up. When released, he appealed for peace and set out to mobilise people across the country. By 1929, the nation was ready again and he returned to active politics through the Indian National Congress. Poorna Swaraj, or Complete Independence, was already a stated goal and Gandhi declared that 'Independence Day' would be celebrated on January 26, a day that is now celebrated as Republic Day.

A year later, he decided to undertake the famous 'salt march' wherein he walked 241 miles from Sabarmati to Dandi along with thousands of enthusiastic supporters. All he did when he reached there was pick up a handful of natural salt, thereby breaking the British government's law that had imposed a tax on the manufacture of salt. He was promptly arrested, and as **Abbas Tyebji** took over the movement, he too was thrown into jail, after which **Sarojini Naidu** was placed in charge. The message went out loud and clear – with or without the physical presence of Gandhi, the fight for independence was well and truly on.

The civil disobedience movement continued even after Gandhi and his most trusted lieutenants, **Jawaharlal Nehru** and **Khan Abdul Gaffar Khan**, were arrested. By 1942, the All India Congress Committee had passed the 'Quit India' resolution and there was a fresh wave of state repression across the country. Kasturba, his wife and partner in all his struggles, died in prison during this time. So did Mahadev Desai, better known as Mahadevbhai, also a former barrister who had served tirelessly as Gandhi's secretary for twenty-five years.

After his release, Gandhi made attempts to negotiate with **Winston Churchill** on the one hand, and with **MA Jinnah**, on the other. Jinnah was now heading the Muslim League that was starting to demand a separate nation. There was little progress until the Second World War ended and the Labour Party came back to power in England. But by 1946, waves of communal violence were sweeping across the subcontinent.

As towns and villages burnt and were pillaged, Gandhi set out on a tour seeking to bring about peace. He succeeded in some places and did not in others. Independence dawned on August 15, 1947 with the dark, brooding clouds of tragic bloodshed and exile on the horizon of what were now two separate nations – India and Pakistan.

After repeated pleas for non-violence, in early 1948, Gandhi started a fast for peace that he described as his greatest. It was also his last.

On January 20th, he narrowly escaped a bomb attack carried out by Madan Lal. However, he appeared unruffled, saying that he would only have proved that he was truly a man of God if he could meet a violent death with a calm countenance and God's name on his lips. On January 30th, when he was on his way to a prayer meeting, Gandhi fell to the bullets fired by Nathuram Godse. His last words were '*Hey, Ram*'.

*Infinite glory of the Lord I praise*
*How can these worldly men know?*
*Protectors of religion, know not you,*
*The difference between gem and stone.*
*Mysterious to Vedas, Gopis access,*
*Very few know the essence of this.*

(Extracted from 'Celebration of Divinity', a collection of Bhakti poems by Narsinh Mehta, the father of Gujarati poetry, and translated by Darshana Trivedi and Rupalee Burke)

Top 1
*Kirti Mandir, Porabandar; Gandhiji's birthplace*

Top 2
*In the courtyard at Sabarmati Ashram, near Ahmedabad*

Left
*Porbandar, the square behind Kirti Mandir, surrounded by doorways on all sides*

Page 14 - Top
*Arrest warrant for the mahatma, 1922; at Sabarmati Ashram*

Page 14 - Bottom
*Always espousing non-violence: telegram from Bapu; at Sabarmati Ashram*

Page 15
*Message from Gandhiji, contemporary even today; Sabarmati Ashram*

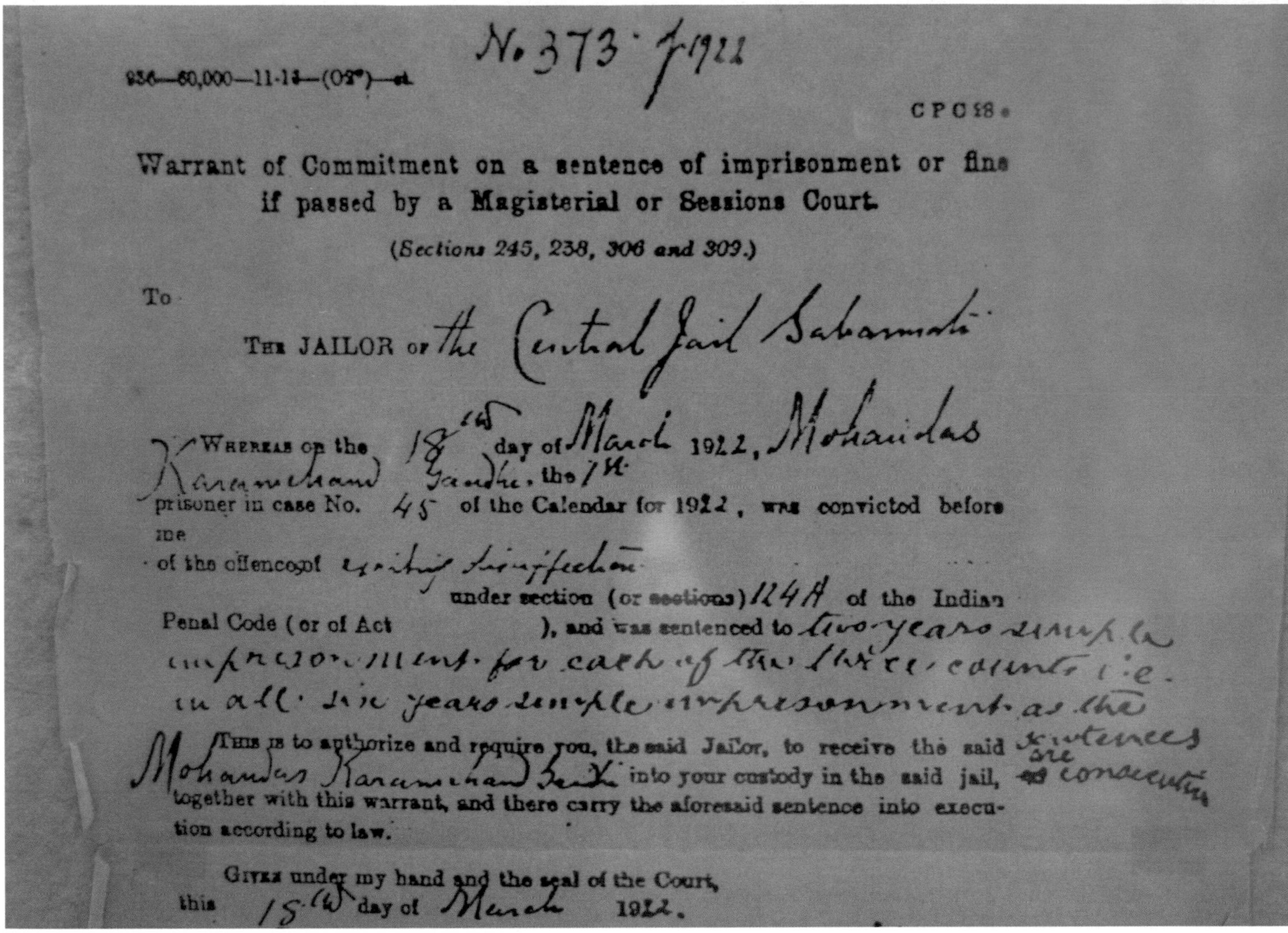

236—60,000—11-13—(02°) at.

CPC18.

## Warrant of Commitment on a sentence of imprisonment or fine if passed by a Magisterial or Sessions Court.

### (Sections 245, 238, 306 and 309.)

To

THE JAILOR OF the *Central Jail Sabarmati*

WHEREAS on the *18th* day of *March* 1922, *Mohandas Karamchand Gandhi*, the *1st* prisoner in case No. *45* of the Calendar for 1922, was convicted before me

of the offence of *exciting disaffection*

under section (or sections) *124A* of the Indian Penal Code (or of Act ), and was sentenced to *two years simple imprisonment for each of the three counts i.e. in all six years simple imprisonment as the sentences are consecutive*

THIS is to authorize and require you, the said Jailor, to receive the said *Mohandas Karamchand Gandhi* into your custody in the said jail, together with this warrant, and there carry the aforesaid sentence into execution according to law.

GIVEN under my hand and the seal of the Court, this *15th* day of *March* 1922.

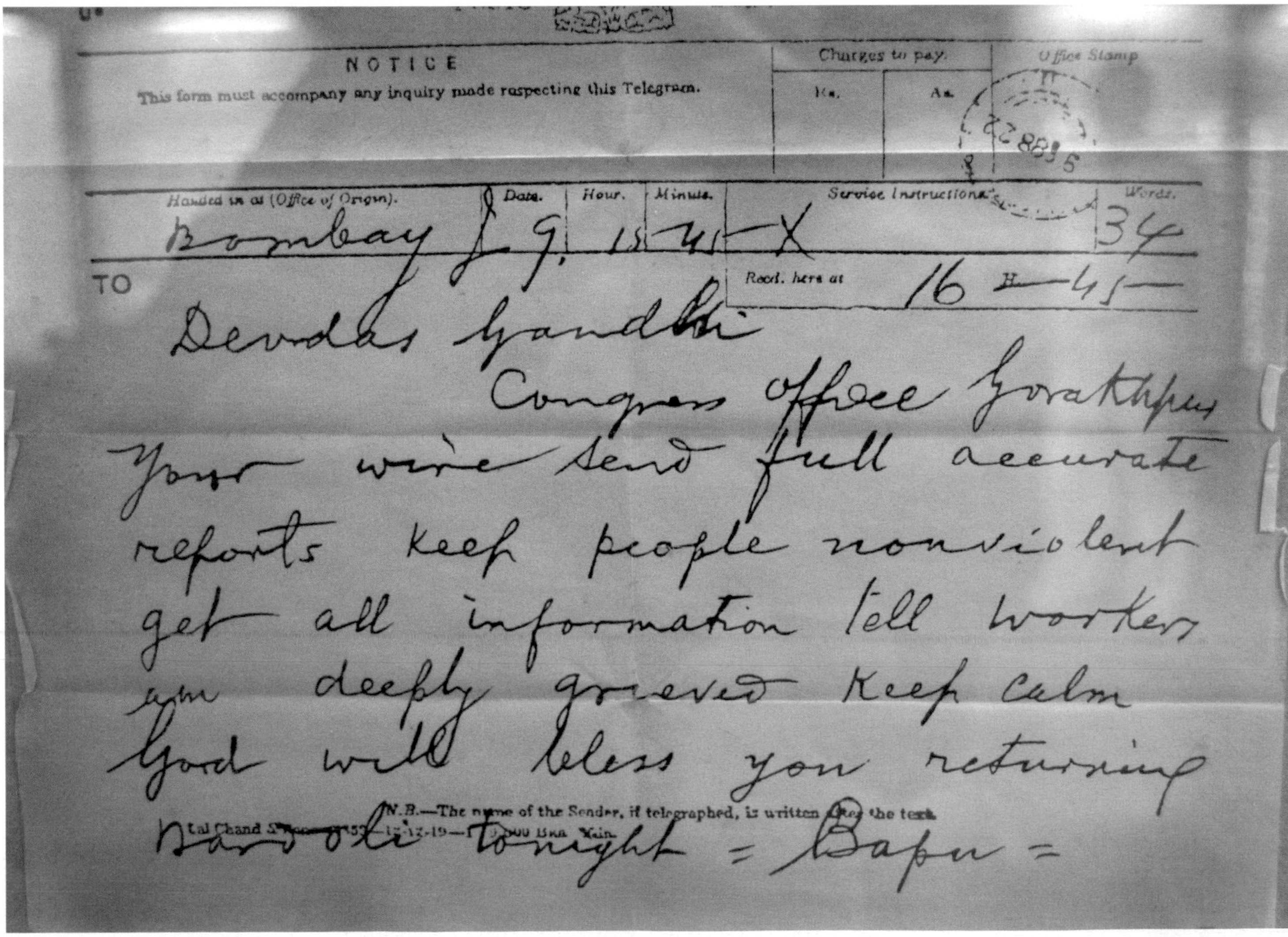

---

| NOTICE | | Charges to pay. | | Office Stamp |
|---|---|---|---|---|
| This form must accompany any inquiry made respecting this Telegram. | | Rs. | As. | |

| Handed in at (Office of Origin). | Date. | Hour. | Minute. | Service Instructions. | Words. |
|---|---|---|---|---|---|
| Bombay | J. 9. | 15 | 41 X | | 34 |

TO Recd. here at 16 H 45

*Devdas Gandhi*

*Congress office Gorakhpur*

*Your wire send full accurate reports keep people nonviolent get all information tell workers am deeply grieved keep calm God will bless you returning*

N.B.—The name of the Sender, if telegraphed, is written over the text.

*tonight = Bapu =*

I will give you a talisman.
Whenever you are in doubt, or when the
self becomes too much with you, apply the
following test. Recall the face of the
poorest and the weakest man whom you may
have seen, and ask yourself, if the step
you contemplate is going to be of any
use to <u>him</u>. Will he gain anything by it ?
Will it restore him to a control over his
own life and destiny ? In other words,
will it lead to Swaraj for the hungry and
spiritually starving millions ?

Then you will find your doubtd
and your self melting away.

# Shaping Gujarat

**Gujarat** was traditionally divided into four zones, along both geographical and socio-cultural lines. Mainland Gujarat, from the tip of the Aravallis to the Western Ghats; the peninsula of Saurashtra or Kathiawad; Kutch and the eastern Adivasi belt, from the Aravallis along the Vindhya-Satpura range down to the Ghats.

Even in the ancient Gupta period, what we now call Gujarat was not one single entity. There were four distinct zones – Anart (north-central), Lat (south), Saurashtra and Kutch. The Adivasi belt was referred to as 'nishad'. Gurjardesh, from which the state's modern name is derived, was only a small area in the north, around Mount Abu.

The state now has the longest coastline amongst all the Indian states. Naturally, it has had several significant ports and a history of international trade. In fact, all the major kingdoms in this region had centered around one major port. These included Bharuch (which was also a junction of the historical silk route and spice route), Khambat, Surat and Bhavnagar. Even today, there are 41 ports, including Kandla, Porbandar and Hazira.

Gujarat, in its present shape, was created only in 1960. After independence, it was divided into three groups – Saurashtra, Kutch and Bombay state. In 1956, Bombay state was enlarged to include the other two. This was a very unpopular move and led to protests based on linguistic identity. In 1960, the whole state was divided into Gujarat and Maharashtra.

Title inset
*Tracing roots to the Harappan civilisation; the main walls of the ancient fort at Dholavira*
Page 26-27
*Excavations of the docks at Lothal; Harappan civilisation*

# The Historic Tale

- First (or what we know thus far to be the first) there was the Indus Valley Civilisation – 2400 BC to 1800 BC.

- The Central Asians, or the Aryans, came in after, with their Vedic culture. According to the Puranas, at least three Aryan tribes – Sharyats, Bhrigus and Yadavs – were part of this wave of migrants.

- From the Ashokan rock edict on the way to Mount Girnar, we gather that Gujarat was a part of the Mauryan and Ashokan empires. Buddhism was probably introduced around that time. When Huien Tsang visited Gujarat in 614 AD, it had more than 150 Buddhist monastries.

- From the 2nd century BC, the Indo-Greeks made an appearance. The Shakas or Scythians and Kushans. Trade between countries and civilisations was as old as Harappa. Even in 4 AD, there were two famous ports known as far away as the Roman Empire – Bhrighukachch (which is now modern Bharuch) and Shurparak (or Sopara).

- In the 5th century AD, came the Huns. Following them, the Gurjars arrived, for whom the state is named.

- In the 8th century AD, the Persian fire worshippers – the Parsis – made an appearance, and sought refuge at Sanjan.

- The Rabari tribes came in via Sind and Rajasthan.

- Until the thirteenth century, the Chalukyas or Solankis ruled, their empire extending from Mewar to Malwa, and the Konkan, including Vasai. During this time, Jainism spread widely. Cambay became a great port – known pretty much as the gateway to Hind. Marco Polo came visiting.

- When Alauddin Khilji beat the last Chalukya king, Gujarat became a part of the Delhi Sultanate.

- The Siddis, of African origin, who may have come either as mercenary soldiers or as slaves, came and settled down here. So did the Turks and Afghans.

- Taimur the Lame invaded the land in the fourteenth century and the Delhi Sultanate disintegrated.

- Soon, the Nazim or Governor of Gujarat declared himself king and thus was founded the Gujarat Sultanate, in 1403.

- From here on, the Ahmedshahi Dynasty took root and began to expand.

- When Cambay declined, due to siltation, Surat began to flourish. European traders arrived in the early sixteenth century.

- The Portuguese came along and tried to fortify the ports where they had trading interests. Diu, remained under Portuguese control until Independence.

- Humayun, the Mughal emperor came warring in 1533. Taking advantage of this diversion, some Rajput warriors also attacked through Kutch. In this way, the Rajput, Jam Rawal established the state of Jamnagar and the Sodha Rajputs established themselves in Saurashtra.

- Emperor Akbar annexed the Gujarat Sultanate in 1572, and it became a 'suba' or province for the next 200 years. Surat, however, was the commercial hub for the Mughals.

- Meanwhile, along the coast, the power struggle went on. The Dutch came in 1606 and the British in 1613, the French in 1668.

- Apart from Ahmedabad and Surat, most modern cities came up during the eighteenth century – for instance, Bhavnagar, Jamnagar, Rajkot, Bhuj.

- This was also the time when the Bhakti and Saint waves swept through the land. Poets, both Hindu and Muslim, laid the foundations for modern Gujarati literature.

- After Aurangzeb and the decline of the Mughal Empire, the Marathas attacked. By the mid-eighteenth century, the Maratha Peshwa and the Gaekwad of Baroda had worked out a revenue-sharing agreement.

- Meanwhile, the smaller kingdoms squabbled. And wherever they could, the British interfered and assumed control. India, as a whole, became a colony.

From *The Shaping of Modern Gujarat*, you could get a crash course in the history of the state.

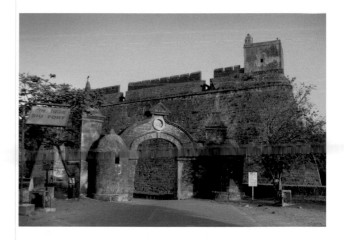

Top
*The Diu Fort*

Right - Top
*Ma - Mother; flying the Indian flag on boats in Chanod. Chanod lies on the banks of the Narmada, and it is believed that while devout Hindus come to wash their sins in the Ganga River, Ganga comes to wash her sins at Chanod*

Right - Bottom
*Annual animal trade fair in Vautha*

*People at the annual animal trade fair in Vautha*

Page 32 - 33
*The Rabaris – Shepherd tribe in Zainabad
– their homes, their work, their food,
leisure and lives; the old and the new
live together and slowly evolve*

Top
*Bhujodi, the Great Rann of Kutch; the charm
of a little Harijan boy, truly a child of God*
Left
*A Rabari in the Little Rann of Kutch*

# The Colonial Yoke

**As India became** a colony, things changed, and amongst other changes, one of the most significant ones was the coming of the railways.

There is a delicious bit of history recorded in the Baroda State Gazetteer (Volume 1), which talks about a time when there was no train in Navsari.

## "Going to Delhi was like visiting another planet."

People would walk or use bullock carts and it took ten days to reach Bombay. And people who went to Bombay rarely, if ever, returned. So, if you had undertaken the journey in, say 1857, your family would wail and weep as if you were dying. The weeping would start the night before, and on the day of the journey, friends would walk with you until the edge of the village.

Now, you could fly into Surat, from Delhi, or Ahmedabad. Even Porbandar has an airport. You're amused at the idea of the look on the faces of people from 1857, if you could have then suggested that they just take the next flight out. Yet, it is something to chew on – if you walk south of Navsari, or hitch rides on the odd cattle-or-camel-cart, after ten days, you could indeed be in Bombay!

**1857**. The year the railways came.

The year of the first war of Indian independence.

Gujarat was central to the freedom movement and was one of the major flag-points during the first war of Indian independence, otherwise known as 'the mutiny'. **Nana Sahib Peshwa**, **Tatiya Tope** and **Maulvi Liaquat Ali** – leaders of the revolt – had ended up taking refuge in this region after the Indian side was beaten.

It is believed that Nana stayed on, as **Swami Dayanand**, in Sihor. Tatiya Tope lived as **Tabel Das** in Navsari and Maulvi Liaquat Ali went to Suchin village before he was arrested and deported.

The other major point of significance about 1857 was the way it changed, for generations to come, the way some groups would be perceived.

There were groups that welcomed the British Raj for their own reasons. This would include much of the elite, merchants who benefitted from the spurt in cotton and opium trade, many rulers of small kingdoms, and many social reformers. Princes, including **Maharaja Khanderao** of Baroda, had extended military support to the British during the 1857 revolt.

**Bapu Gaekwad**, a rebel prince, had planned to attack Baroda during Diwali, but someone leaked the plan and the rebels were arrested. Bapu Gaekwad survived, but many others were blown up or hung or sent to the Andamans. The talukdars had begun to resist the British when the annual levies got too high for comfort.

Apart from the Thakors, the most resistant groups were tribals who fought bitterly for their independence and their rights over land and natural resources. In fact, they continued to fight until 1859, using guerrilla warfare tactics.

Title inset
*Swimming pool at Rajkumar College, Rajkot*

Top 1
*At the exclusive platform in Gondal, the maharaja's railway carriage*

Top 2
*The sitting room in the royal train*

Left
*The personal salon in the maharaja's private train, Gondal*

The Bhils of eastern Gujarat, the Mahi Kantha and Rewa Kantha, the Kolis and Vaghers in the Gir forests continued to resist. Near Dwarka, in an area called Okhamandal, in 1858, the Vagher revolt was led by **Jodha Manek**.

Colonial forces eventually recaptured the area and the people were forcibly disarmed, which was a severe blow to these traditional hunters. The tribal groups paid an extra-heavy price for their resistance. They were declared outlaws, classified as 'criminal tribes' and for decades to come, were treated not like heroic warriors but like common criminals.

**The reclamation** of tribal dignity has not been easy; even now, the course remains an uphill one. But people have tried. People such as **Dr Devy**, who founded the **Bhasha Institute** in Baroda.

The institute documents and researches tribal art, literature and related traditions. It has also set up a Tribal Training Institute in Tejgarh with a special focus on water and grain banks, gene banks, micro-credit and artists' co-operatives. Young students are trained through non-formal methods, in their own dialects, about their own constitutional rights, minimum wages, health and perhaps, most importantly, themselves.

One of the publications the institute brings out is '*Dhol*', a magazine printed in eleven languages – Rathwi, Dungri Bhili, Panchmahali Bhili, Gor Banjara, Bhantu, Dehwali, Pawri, Kukna, Choudhari, Ahirani and Marathi.

Bhasha has also set up the Denotified Tribes Rights Action Group (DNT-RAG), with a newsletter called '*Budhan*', named after a young man who died in police custody.

(For more on Bhasha, Dhol and Budhan, visit www.bhasharesearch.org)

# All rulers fall. All dynasties end. There was no reason for the British rule to be any different.

**Gandhinagar** is now the capital of Gujarat. A relatively new city, it is also one of the few 'planned' cities of India. Set up along the Sabarmati river, the city is the administrative centre. It is also emerging as a new educational hub, thanks to the scarcity of land in Ahmedabad.

**Rajkot** was founded in 1612 by Vibhaji Ajoji Jadeja of the Jadeja Dynasty, who was descended from Jam Sataji of Nawanagar, now called Jamnagar. Soon after India's independence, when Saurashtra was still a separate state, Rajkot was its capital.

One of Rajkot's most famous sons is Mahatma Gandhi, who had spent his childhood in Rajkot for his father was a Diwan to the ruler. The house where he lived has been converted into a museum: *Kaba Gandhi No Delo*. The school he attended – Alfred High School is now called Mahatma Gandhi High School.

Visitors cannot miss the majestic doorway with a clock which leads into the ancient Morbi market. Rajkot also boasts of an exotic palace not far from the main city – the Palace of Wankaner, today a heritage hotel and a place renowned for its scenic beauty.

Rajkot city today is mostly known for its small-scale manufacturing industries, such as bearings, diesel engines, kitchen knives and other appliances.

*If he (a king) oppresses people, pauperizes them and favours the subjects in one area so that they may become wealthy at the expense and pauperisation of subjects in another area, the people must rise against such a king and the kingdom must be handed over to another king.*

**Durgaram,** one of founders of Manav Dharmsabha, in 1844, after the salt-tax strike.

Top
*Assembly hall at Rajkumar college*

Left - Top
*Wankaner, the royal coat of arms*

Left - Bottom
*The Palace at Wankaner - an era lingers on*

Page 40
*Wankaner, royal transportation of yore*

Page 41
*The strong and upright heritage of Vijay Vilas Palace, Mandvi. Made entirely of sandstone, the imposing building preserves magnificent art forms within its architecture*

Page 42
*Pragya Mahal, Bhuj*

Page 43
*Standing guard at the fascinating perspective of arched openings at Wankaner Palace*

Top
*The magnificent Laxmi Vilas Palace at
Vadodara is an amazing mix of various
types of architectural styles - Indo-Saracenic,
Gothic, European, traditional Indian*

Left
*Wankaner Palace; you can see the
huge main spiral under reconstruction
to capture its old glory*

Page 44 - Bottom
*Porbandar, the relatively new summer palace
of the maharaja. By the sea, this building
too is now decrepit and unoccupied*

Page 46-47
*The imposing palace at Jamnagar, where
today, just one man lives, the descendant
of a renowned royal family*

The land is **rich** with sacrifice; it resounds with hundred different strains on the **melody** of truth.

# Words, Weapons

**It goes beyond** the Mahatma. Beyond those who fought and died. It is rich with those who were also willing to fight the enemy within, those who fought with ideas, against ideas.

**Narmad,** for instance. Native of Surat, student of Elphinstone College, outspoken journalist and activist; one of the best-known poets, and compiler of the first Gujarati lexicon: *Narmakosh*; author of *Rajyarang*, almost a history of civilisations spanning five thousand years.

This man was thrown out of his caste when he married a widow. A Nagar Brahmin himself, he had long been an advocate of widow remarriages.

One of Narmad's contemporaries and a fellow-Surati called **Mahipatram** had been confronted with a similar fate when he went to England for higher studies. In those days, sea voyages were forbidden for the upper castes and if you did go, you had to perform 'prayaschit', or a ritual penance, to be allowed re-entry into the caste fold (even Gandhiji had to). When Mahipatram was expelled from the caste, he faced an awful prospect; his father died but no Brahmin was willing to perform the last rites. His will was broken under such pressure, and he bowed to the wishes of his caste. He performed the penance and re-entered his caste but later wrote an article expressing his real views on the subject of foreign travel. He was expelled a second time. After four years, Mahipatram once again buckled and once again performed the penance rituals which allowed him to re-enter the caste.

Narmad, now described as Veer Narmad, was made of sterner stuff; he never apologised and never buckled under pressure. As a result, he died an outcast. And yet, how much he must have loved his homeland – to have written of Gujarat with such devotion and pride as is evidenced in the poem:

જય જય ગરવી ગુજરાત!
જય જય ગરવી ગુજરાત,
દીપે અરુણું પરભાત,
ધ્વજ પ્રકાશશે ઝળળળ કસુંબી, પ્રેમ શૌર્ય અંકિત;
તુ ભણાવ ભણાવ નિજ સંતાજિ સઉને, પ્રેમ ભક્તિની રીત –
ઊંચી તુજ સુંદર જાત,
જય જય ગરવી ગુજરાત.
ઉત્તરમાં અંબા માત,
પૂરવમાં કાળી માત,
છે દક્ષિણ દિશામાં કરંત રક્ષા, કુંતેશ્વર મહાદેવ;
ને સોમનાથ ને દ્વારકેશ એ, પશ્ચિમ કેરા દેવ–
છે સહાયમાં સાક્ષાત
જય જય ગરવી ગુજરાત.
નદી તાપી નર્મદા જોય,
મહી ને બીજિ પણ જોય.
વળી જોય સુભટના જુદ્ધ રમણને, રત્નાકર સાગર;
પર્વત પરથી વીર પૂર્વજો, હે આશિષ જયકર –
સંપે સોયે સઉ જાત,
જય જય ગરવી ગુજરાત.
તે અણહિલવાડના રંગ,
તે સિદ્ધરાજ જયસિંગ.
તે રંગ થકી પણ અધિક સરસ રંગ, થશે સત્વરે માત!
શુભ શકુન દીસે મધ્યાહ્ન શોભશે, વીતી ગઈ છે રાત.
જન ઘૂમે નર્મદા સાથ,
જય જય ગરવી ગુજરાત.

*Kabir, Kalidas, Mirabai. All these poets are counted as 'Gujarati'. We hear their dohas, bhajans, though they were written originally in another language. Gujarati and other Indian languages had common roots. A thousand years ago, there was a common maru-gurjar language in this belt, for which manuscripts are still preserved in Khambat, Kutch and Patan. The oral tradition simply tweaked the language and incorporated the poetry.*

Rajendra Shukla, poet.

Title inset
*Bharuch, 150-year-old bridge made of steel*
Left
*The proud, patriotic, brilliant waves of fishing boat flags at Okha*

Narmad is generally acknowledged as the father of modern Gujarati prose. Like all other Indian languages, Gujarati too is a relatively new tongue and is still evolving. Yet, it is already stamped with a distinctive ethos, bearing the tell-tale marks of those who speak her.

If Urdu grew as the language of the camp, Gujarati was the language of the bazaar – flexible in the way she drew words from sailors, traders and merchants, unstintingly. From the humble 'batata' to the mish-mashed 'makkarba': words here weren't bought or sold. They were just picked up and taken home. Like 'pagaar', the Portuguese for salary which is used all over Gujarat and Maharashtra.

## A fluid language that comes from a fluid people - always moving, always shifting.

**In India**, sixty percent of the people are migrants of some sort. Gujarat tops this list; almost seventy percent of the communities living here have migrated from somewhere else. Of the 289 communities listed, 186 were Hindu, of which 124 were migrants. Out of 87 Muslim communities, 67 were migrants. Of the 13 Jain communities, 12 were migrants. All were hunter-gatherers, seventy percent of the fisherfolk, seventy percent of the agriculturalists and fifty percent of the artisan communities believe that they migrated to Gujarat.

According to legend, even Lord Krishna had come here – to Dwarka – from the north. A divine migrant amongst migrants.

Perhaps that is the key to that well-known trait: adaptability.

When people move, they learn to adapt – quickly and without remorse.

Gujaratis are known for their ability to deal with change, for being able to adapt. You have been told that over and over, and then you see it too. You see it in curious ways, like when you go shopping for the traditional 'kaapda' or the backless choli that Kutchi women wear; you realise just how fast the tradespeople adapt, and how complete a change can be when you cannot find what you want for love or for money; there is no example of the traditional backless blouse to be found in the local markets outside of Kutch. The backless 'kaapda' has undergone a slight metamorphosis. It has developed – strips of cloth on both sides of the bodice; the strings have multiplied; it is shorter in front. The embroidery patterns have shifted from rounded emphasis on the twin assets on the front of the choli to plentiful beads and mirrors down the sleeves and on Sindhi caps that even some women wear during Navratri. The pattern of the choli, naturally, meets the demand. Now that the demand has moved on, the suppliers have moved on too; they waste little time or money on stocking nostalgia. In fact, there is no overwhelming regret surrounding the disappearance of what things were like earlier. Change is all around, and people are always finding ways out of one thing and into another.

Top
*The ubiquitous and always evolving 'choli'*
Left - Top
*Riding high at Porbandar*
Left - Bottom
*...and riding together across the ancient land*

# Stitched Into Time

**Patan Patola** is one of those nostalgia-inducing objects of incredible beauty and skill. What was special about this particular silk was that the fabric was woven from pre-dyed threads and that there was not a single knot anywhere. All the different threads to be used were dyed in their appropriate colours before the weaving began. If there was a single mistake, or a thread broke, the whole cloth would have to be unraveled and the weaver would begin all over again.

## Now, the Patan patola is barely alive. There is only one family left in Patan that knows how to weave the exquisite patola the way it used to be done centuries ago.

The weavers of patola, according to legend, were reluctant migrants to the kingdom of Patan. It is believed that a king called Kumarpal was in the habit of donning a new patola dress every single day. He never repeated a costume. The patola was then woven in Jalna. One day, Kumarpal discovered, or suspected, that the king of Jalna had been sending him used robes. He decided to declare war, a war that he won eventually. Later, he had seven hundred weavers brought over from Jalna to his capital and thus started the tradition of the Patan patola.

There is no way of knowing whether the patolas available today are made using this stringent technique, but they certainly are priced as though they are every bit the authentic thing, and they look as good.

**Wlloo Mirza** has worked for years to keep the rich textile traditions from dying out. She's been associated with Gurjari, NID, NIFT, Shreyas and now SEVA.

In this latest avataar, she is helping to bridge the gap between the market and the craftspeople. The textiles or fabrics are produced in urban areas, and taken to rural areas for 'value addition'; that is, for embroidery, mirror-work and other kinds of embellishments. She estimates that about three thousand women are connected with the effort, across forty-five villages in Banaskantha and Kutch.

Mirza was a student of Fine Arts at MS University, Baroda. As a student, she visited the Calico Museum and decided that that would be her line of work. She was fascinated by the fact that "Ahmedabad was once the Manchester of the East. Fabrics used to be exported far from here, even to Indonesia."

And, then she goes on about other craft forms – *mata ni pachedi*, lacquer-work, *rogan* (a kind of trailing technique using castor-oil based colours), quilt-making, patchwork and the very distinctive Parsi embroidery.

She rues the fact that some of the best weavers are not sharing their knowledge with the wider community, which might help the techniques survive. "There is a very small community in Patan that does the patola. But they don't share their knowledge so easily. The patola is now very expensive, of course. The original authentic patola used to cost Rs 25,000 in the 1980s, but now the range starts at Rs 1.3 lakh. We have

> *Mashru was this incredible fabric that arose from a social-religious taboo. Muslims, it is alleged, were not allowed to wear pure silk. So the weavers solved the problem by inventing a form of weaving with both cotton and silk threads so that the silk layer remains on the outside and does not touch the skin, while cotton remains underneath. It was a sort of double weave with very vibrant colours... nowadays, there are efforts to revive mashru, but people don't use pure silk. They use rayon.*

**Wiloo Mirza,** textile designer and developer

Title inset
*Threads woven into the life of Pithapur*

Top
*Pithapur; weaving stunning sarees for the whole country in an age-old tradition*

Left
*Dipped in deep colours to create a rich and beautiful art; a dyer's tell-tale hand*

Page 54 - Top Left
*Tying the knots; a bandhini (tie & dye) creator in Jamnagar*

Page 54 - Top Right
*The cloth, once it is all tied and ready for dyeing*

Page 54 - Bottom Left
*Deep into the dye*

Page 64 - Bottom Right
*...and drying the final garment*

Page 55
*Bubble and boil; much heat and sweat goes into making the attractive fabric you buy*

set up a Rashtriya Shala in Rajkot to teach weaving, but still, the patola is increasingly rare."

But there are people trying to change that, too. Amongst those making a concerted effort at revival is **Asif Sheikh**.

An Ahmedabad-based designer, Asif recognises that quality work – very refined, very delicate work done by human hands – is a luxury. The more exquisite embroidery had always needed rich patrons. In the absence of maharaos and nawabs, it flailed and very nearly disappeared. But, Asif now concentrates on taking the fine craft practices back to the elite.

The bandhini work in Gujarat is distinctive for the finesse of its work, for the smallness of its knots and the detail of tiny dot-like patterns. The best sample of this work in contemporary times lies in **Dawood Kaka**'s hands.

He lives right opposite the Darya Pir Dargah (the tomb of the patron saint of the fishermen and sailors in this region: the saint of the sea) and carries on a mission less spiritual, more temporal, but nonetheless demanding of faith. Dawood Kaka is a legendary craftsman and the winner of a national award for his bandhini work.

It is said that the award-winning saree is now reserved for special visits. If you were to ask him nicely, he just might open one single knot for you.

If Asif can make good his claim – about training artisans to do the sort of work that matches anything you see in the Calico Museum – he may well succeed in taking your breath away.

One thing does take your breath away. An exceptionally delicate piece of 'mochi kaam' in the Calico Museum at Ahmedabad. Off-white thread on off-white fabric. While it looks graceful enough as it is, you need to see it against the light to feel the strange impact a piece of cloth can have on a human soul. It is hard to find words for a moment in which a shadowy bit of embroidered cloth begins to speak. This was one of the pieces commissioned by the Portuguese, perhaps for a chapel, and when the fabric is held up against a pale yellow light – ideally, candlelight, or maybe the dim natural light of the early mornings or dusk, the bit of embroidered fabric comes alive. In the interplay of light and dark, the pattern stands out, clearly defined, almost as an idea showing itself or a mind being illuminated.

As the museum staff dims the lights and shows you this piece, all you can do is take in a deep, startled breath and exhale with a sigh and an 'Oh!' If a piece of cloth could ever impress upon you the glory of creation, imbue you with a spiritual melancholy or bathe your eyes in a reverent silence, it is this.

At the Calico Museum, the guide tells you that her name means 'lady of the lotus'. **Kamalini**. In other words, Lakshmi.

Lakshmi and Ahmedabad are rumoured to have an eternal, mythic relationship. The story goes thus: Once upon a time, long ago, a guard at Bhadra gate (Ahmedabad had 12 gates) saw a woman leaving the city late at night. He stopped her and asked her who she was and where she was going. She told him that she was Lakshmi, the goddess of wealth and prosperity. The guard was faced with a dilemma; how could he let Lakshmi leave his city? So, he asked her to wait until he returned; he would go to the king and get permission. However, he realised that the city must never be separated from prosperity, and so he decided not to return at all. He killed himself and Lakshmi stayed on.

Kamalini 'lady-of-the-lotus', guide at the museum, is a no-nonsense type. She tells a fascinating story about the origin of the *booti*. "What you call the *booti*, (the curving oval with a tapering end) was actually an *Adivasi* motif. To celebrate and to express their joy after a plentiful harvest, the tribals made white rice-paste and stamped their fists side-ways to make an imprint. It was a symbol of fertility. Of joy and plenty."

*I can guarantee that the quality of work I am getting our artisans to do now can match anything you see in the Calico Museum. We are using all the traditional stitches. The mochi kaam was the most common one - a kind of 'aari' or chain stitch. Then there was mirror work, called 'abhla', bead work or moti kaam, cord work or dori kaam. Appliqué, patchwork and Khadi prints in gold and silver, Ajrak, Kimkhab are the others. There is also a form of embroidery called 'Soof'. It came from the region that has now gone to Pakistan – that side of Kutch; it looked like miniature phulkari. The best fabrics were the patola from Patan, mashru, and bandhini. The Gujarati Bandhini work is much finer than the one you see in Rajasthan.*

**Asif Sheikh,** Textile designer

Top 1
*The lacquered designs of the Sankheda furniture from the south of Gujarat, near Vadodara*

Top 2
*An Ahir woman poses proudly, happily, next to her gleaming and colourful dowry*

Left - Top
*Patiently, persistently the carver carves a block with a clear eye and a delicacy of touch. Pithapur, near Ahmedabad, creates blocks for textile printing for almost the entire country. It is an art, a craft, a livelihood here*

Left - Bottom
*The block-carver's tool kit*

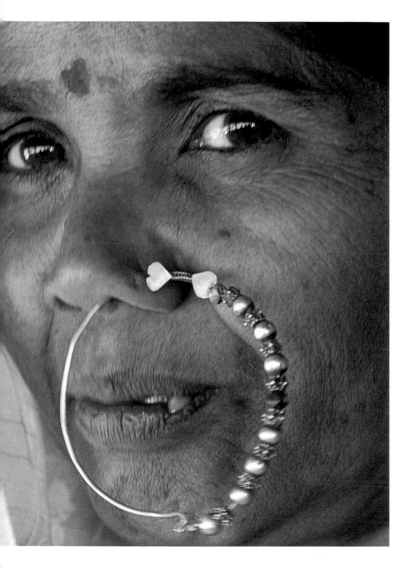

Painting has been a part of the people's daily life. They painted their own walls, even the horns of their cattle. Gujaratis have always been huge consumers. They have always used the bulk of what they made, and that is why many of the crafts did not die out. The ones that required rich patrons are almost gone. There are attempts at revival, however, there is a difference. Earlier, the craftsman was also the designer. The motifs, the colours, were of his own choice. Now, he or she will make what the designers demand. Craft as a form of self-expression is limited.

Painting has been a part of the people's daily life. They painted their own walls, even the horns of their cattle. Gujaratis have always been huge consumers. They have always used the bulk of what they made, and that is why many of the crafts did not die out. The ones that required rich patrons are almost gone. There are attempts at revival, however, there is a difference. Earlier, the craftsman was also the designer. The motifs, the colours, were of his own choice. Now, he or she will make what the designers demand. Craft as a form of self-expression is limited.

# River Bank
## Boomtown

**Ahmedabad**, or what the average Gujarati calls Amdavad is named after its founder, **Ahmed Shah**. The city was founded in 1411, the new capital of the Sultanate of Gujarat, although it is said that the area around had been inhabited since the eleventh century. When **Karandev I**, a Solanki king who ruled from the area that corresponds to present-day Patan, defeated the Bhil king of Ashaval, he established a city called **Karnavati**, which was near the Sabarmati River. After the Solanki rulers were edged out by the Vaghelas from Dholka, the capital was conquered by the rulers from Delhi.

In 1411, the Muzaffarid dynasty was in power in this part of Gujarat. Legend has it that Ahmed Shah was camping on the banks of the Sabarmati when he saw a hare chasing a dog. Impressed by the unusual courage on display, the king decided that he would build his new capital here, in a place where even the hares were so brave!

In 1487, **Mahmud Begada** (Mahmud, conqueror of two forts) the grandson of Ahmed Shah, began to fortify the city. It had an outer wall running about ten kilometres and had twelve gates. The Muzaffarids lost Ahmedabad in 1573, when the Mughal emperor Akbar wrested control of the region. During this time, Ahmedabad became one of the biggest centres of trade. Shahjahan spent the prime of his life in this city, and built the Moti Shahi Mahal in Shahibaug during his stay. The Mughals lost Ahmedabad to the Marathas eventually. But, a terrible famine in 1630 was made worse by the looting and in-fighting of the Marathas, as a result of which large parts of the city were ruined, and many citizens were forced to flee.

Eventually, the British took over from the Marathas in 1818, and went about modernising the infrastructure. The city benefitted from the introduction of modern textile technology and was soon the booming centre of the textile industry in India. Often called the Manchester of the East, Ahmedabad produces the largest amount of denim in the world.

The first Gujarati to set up a cotton textile mill in Ahmedabad was **Ranchhodlal Chhotalal**. His story is a very interesting one. Success was never uniformly his; nor was the moral high ground. He was a bureaucrat who was dismissed on charges of corruption before he took to business. At first, he couldn't get the financial backing but in 1861, he found the money to set up the first textile mill in what is now officially demarcated as Gujarat.

Title inset
*IIM-A; silhouette of the Indian Institute of Management, Ahmedabad*

Top
*The first Gujarati to set up a cotton textile mill in Ahmedabad was Ranchhodlal Chhotalal*

Left - Top
*Teen Darwaza - three doors - gateways to the old city of Ahmedabad*

Left - Bottom
*The universally recognised 'jaali' with the intricately carved Tree of Life, located in a mosque in the centre of a traffic roundabout in Ahmedabad*

Top and Left

*Sarkhej Roza, outside Ahmedabad, is an elegant early example of Indo-Saracenic architecture. Built at the end of the Sultanate era, the complex has mosques, pavilions, retreats and tombs in a campus that combined religious, social and royal spaces in harmony. Efforts are being made to restore and develop the complex as a social and cultural hub*

Top and Left
*Devotees at Swaminarayan
Mandir, Ahmedabad; a vibrant and
colourful testament to faith*

71

Top
*Calligraphed name of Allah at the
Jami Masjid in Ahmedabad*
Left
*The faithful at Jami Masjid in Ahmedabad*

There are **spaces**
for night in this city.
**Spaces** where you not
only bow at peace,
or in grief, but to
escape. **Spaces** of
cleaning, not only of
the hands and feet but
also of the head.
Large open **spaces**
and still, green waters.
Green graces.
And Sunday mornings.

**Manek Chowk**, one of the capital's busiest spaces, would not have existed at all, if the man after whom it is named, had had his way. Ahmedabad itself would not have existed.

The story is so fantastic, so touched by magic that you want to believe it.

**Baba Manek**, apparently, was a sadhu with magical powers, and he was intent on thwarting the then king's plans to build a new capital east of the Sabarmati River. Everyday, as the builders would raise the new fortress' walls, this Baba would sit quietly, weaving a mat. At night, he would unravel his weaving, and the fortress' walls would come crashing down!

The king, however, was a determined man and a clever one. When he heard about the Baba, he sent for him and asked him to prove that he indeed had magical powers, by entering into a jar. Baba Manek did so, and just as quickly, the jar was stopped up and buried.

The capital city got built after all. But the king did not forget the powerful sadhu. He laid the foundation stone of Ahmedabad in a bastion called Manek Burj.

One of the special characteristics of Ahmedabad is her several streets that specialise in certain professions or products. Paldi is one area that has many shops selling embroidery from Kutch and Saurashtra. Rangeela pol is where many artisans create colourful bandhinis (tie and-dye work). Madhupura is known for the traditional *mojris* (shoes). Idols of various deities can be found in Gulbai Tekra. Rows of makeshift stalls outside Law Garden are a major attraction, for they sell a lot of mirror work clothes and jewellery.

Even today, Ahmedabad is one of the largest industrial centres in the western part of India. It has a growing chemicals and pharmaceuticals industry and two of the biggest pharmaceutical companies in India are based here.

There is an interesting mix of architectural styles within the city. Sultan Ahmed Shah's kingdom introduced the Indo-Saracenic style still witnessed in the surviving monuments and mosques. There are ancient step-wells, a unique feature of the area, and ornately carved temples. Modern Ahmedabad boasts of buildings by famous architects – **Louis Kahn**, **Le Corbusier**, **Charles Correa** and **BV Doshi**.

*The business-mindedness of Gujaratis finds itself reflected in architecture as well. The kings and other rich builders would use the most economic options while building. There was never an outright, visible attempt to establish identity through their buildings. The local rulers would patronise local craftsmen. They chose the cheapest available labour and the craftsmen brought in their own traditions and techniques to the construction. That is how you find Jain influences in a mosque. The syncretism, whether it is in architecture or elsewhere, is a result of pragmatic, economic decisions.*

*Ahmedabad is a modern, industrial city. And it has always had lots of money. Corbusier, the French architect, found his first clients not in Delhi, but here in Ahmedabad. Also, there is a culture of design here. The Ahmedabad School of Architecture is the nation's most dynamic, most credible one. There are several urban planners here. In fact, some of Gujarat's planners in the 1980s made genuine attempts at bringing about a measure of urban equity.*

Jagan Shah, architect

Wagh Bakri House

Top 1
*Law Gardens, Ahmedabad; Gujarati jewellery is famous throughout the country and today it adapts itself to the fashion that sweeps cinema and television*

Top 2
*Wagh Bakri House, Ahmedabad; Wagh Bakri is the tea that Gujaratis drink. It is also the second largest tea-seller in the country and the company is owned by Piyush Bhai Desai*

Left - Top
*The popular food stalls at Manek Chowk, Ahmedabad*

Left - Bottom
*Bling sells! At Law Gardens - the buzzing hub of Ahmedabad evenings*

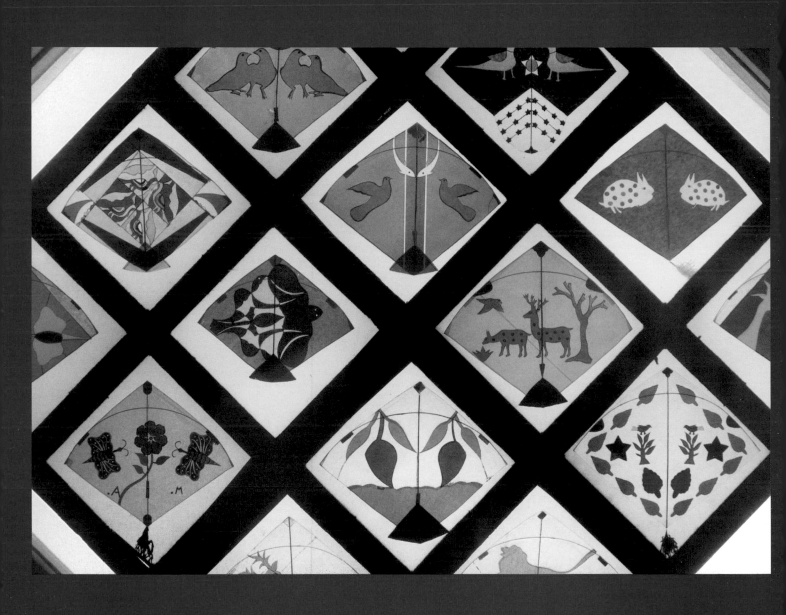

Page 80
*The angles and arches, the colourful
intricacies that decorate the
Swaminarayan Mandir, Ahmedabad*

Page 81
*A play of light and shadow in the modern
sweep of the geometric lines of the
prestigious IIM-A, built by Louis Kahn*

Top
*The architectural variation and experiments
in Gujarat are a tradition inherited and
continued. The Gufa (Cave) is a modern,
artistic, almost surreal structure designed
by BV Doshi and the artist, MF Hussain*

Left
*The rampant kite-flying and innovative kite
creations have led to a whole museum dedicated
to kites; the Kite Museum, Ahmedabad*

Page 84-85
*Vishalla, the Utensil Museum, Ahmedabad*
*– traditional water vessels, rolling*
*pins, kitchen utensils - a cornucopia of*
*unexpected and captivating objects*

Top and Right
*Quiet lives around the silent old*
*darwazas of the old city, Ahmedabad*

**According to** Hindu mythology, Sati, the first wife of Lord Shiva, killed herself because she could not bear the way her father was insulting her husband. Once she committed suicide, Shiva was so enraged that he would not perform her last rites. He picked up her dead body on his shoulder and in an uncontrollable fit of grief and fury he danced a terrible *tandav*, his divine dance of destruction. As the whole world was threatened, the Lord of Preservation decided to calm him down. He cut Sati's body into fifty-one bits and it fell at fifty-one different places. Where her broken heart fell – that spot is called **Ambaji.**

Located in Mehsana, about 70 kms from Ahmedabad, the 900-year old Sun Temple at **Modhera** is a famous and fine specimen of Indian temple architecture, every inch of which is covered with magnificent carvings of the gods, flowers, animals and erotic sculptures. The stunning and partially ruined Sun Temple was built by king **Bhimdev I** of the Solanki Rajput clan. The design ensured that the Sun, as it rose at the equinoxes, shone on the image of Surya, the Sun God. A pillared porch leads to the main hall and shrine.

The Rani Udaymati Vav, one of the largest step wells in Gujarat built in the eleventh century is adorned with over 800 stone sculptures and reliefs – images of Gods of the Hindu pantheon.

Well known around the area for the Mehsani buffalo and the large Dudhsagar co-operative milk dairy, Mehsana also has other Jain temples and a temple of Mata Bechraji.

Title inset
*Steps leading to the Surya Kund
(tank) in front of the temple*

Top
*Young visitors in the Sabha
Mandap of the temple*

Left
*Built in the 11c. by the Solanki dynasty,
the temple was so designed that the first
rays of the sun fell on the image of Surya,
the Sun God, at the time of equinoxes*

Page 90 - Top and Bottom
*Hatheesinh Jain Temple, outside Delhi Gate,
Ahmedabad, built in 1850 by a rich Jain
merchant. It is made purely of marble and
is one of Ahmedabad's famed tourist sites*

Page 91 - Top
*Palitana Jain Temple complex, enroute
from Bhavnagar to Diu. 863 Jain temples
are perched in a cluster on top of a hill; you
climb 3000 steps to see this architectural,
aritistic and religious marvel*

Page 91 - Bottom
*The first mandir as you enter
the Palitana complex*

Top
*Meant for three, but the more the
merrier is the common rule*

Left
*Not often that you see an empty patch of road
in this vegetable bazaar at Surat where the
long narrow lane between buildings bustles
with customers crowding to pick the day's best*

# Prosperity and the Port

**From the joy** of the tribal heart blessed with a good harvest, to printing blocks and looms and sarees, the *booti* is everywhere.

## In Surat, the sarees are everywhere.

Surat, a port city on the banks of the River Tapti, is the second largest city in the state.

Until the thirteenth century, it was still a village, according to the travelogues of Arab visitors from that era. By the fifteenth century, it was a well-established port town, especially made prosperous after the decline of the port of Cambay or Khambat.

By the sixteenth century, the Portuguese had established themselves at Surat and following in their trail, the East India Company, from England. By the seventeenth century, Surat was a wealthy city which drew the attentions of Shivaji and his Maratha forces, who repeatedly sacked the city and carried off the plunder. Over the last century, with the damming of the Tapti, sea trade became impossible.

Fires, floods and plagues have visited this city time and again, causing terrible damage even in recent decades.

The remarkable thing about Surat is that it has always clawed its way back to prominence as a centre of trade and manufacture, though the industries have changed form. From sailing and shipbuilding to cotton and paper mills and then again, to polyester and diamonds. One in every five sarees in the country is made in Surat now, and the city remains the most important centre for diamond cutting and polishing in India.

Surat. A city about which a travel agent will warn you: "Madam, frankly, there is nothing here. Only business."

Fancy then, that, you should walk right into the belly of this buzzing business city, and bump into a poet!

Not a poet wandering about, passing through, looking at scurrying, scampering feet bearing ten-kilo *potlas* on migrant shoulders, or pondering over the steady grace of teenaged girls' fingers, turning sheets of cardboard into neat boxes, into which the waiting yards of fabric will be folded, packed, bought, gifted.

No, this is a poet who deals in 'gray cloth' or 'kaccha maal'. Which is actually white cloth – the un-dyed, un-printed material that is brought to the textile market from the polyester units, and is sent on to other smaller units – to be designed, cut, embroidered and embellished, before it returns here – to one of the 125 textile markets in Surat, which supplies one in every five sarees sold in this nation.

This is the city that churns out twenty-eight percent of the total synthetic fibre in India. And the poet is a cog in the powerloom.

Title inset
*Fishing boats on their way to Surat*

Top 1
*Bandhini sarees at Tribal Haat*

Top 2
*Polyester riding pillion through the marketplace*

Left
*No woman can quite resist the lure of the Surati saree; customers at an open saree shop in Surat*

**Ramesh Shayar**: poet, teacher from Anand, traces his lineage to Haryana, 'gray-broker', and now, Bollywood lyricist.

Between talk of POY (Partially Oriented Yarn) and powerlooms (each manufacturing unit has 72 looms, 8 lakh looms, they're guessing), gray cloth (800 dyeing and printing houses), Reliance polymer chips, fashion (no flowers, all fancy geometric patterns) and 'raksha-bandhan' demand (cheaper sarees), sequins and Chinese *maal*, Ramesh Shayar will show off the stills and publicity photos from the forthcoming film *'Humraah - the traitor'* for which he has written the songs.

The proprietor of the wholesale shop, Varun, a young man in his twenties, will brief you on his view of Gujarati society. "There are 4 types of people in Gujarat. Pure Gujaratis, Surati, Kathiawadi and Saurashtra-people. Pure Gujaratis are traders like me. Suratis are traditionally very happy-go-lucky. If they earn four thousand, they spend four thousand. No tension in life. We are the ones who save up and also get stressed about money."

Surat, he says, is industrial and industrious.

"Outsiders make money easily over here. The most successful wholesalers in the textile market are Sindhis, Marwaris and Punjabis. But the most hard-working are Kathiawadis. If needed, the owner of the shop will lift the *potla* himself; even if he is a *crorepati*, he will not mind lifting a load."

An Urdu poet once waxed eloquent about his favourite city by saying that his heart finds no peace when it is separated from Surat.

अग़र देखे हैं लोगन शाम–ऐ–तबरेज
न देखा कोई एसा मुल्क–ए–ज़रखेज
के इस भीतर कई ऐसे हैं तुज्जर
के करूं कोन नहीं उन के नजिक बार ...
भरी है सीरत ओ सूरत से सूरत
हर इक सूरत है वहां अनमोल मूरत
ख़त्म है अम्रादन ऊपर सफाई
वाली है बिस्तर हुस्न–ऐ निसा

*(People may have seen Syria and Tabriz,*
*But no one has seen such a prosperous place.*
*For in it, there are such merchants*
*To whom Croesus could not measure up ...*
*Surat is filled with (fine) reputations and faces,*
*Every face there is a priceless idol.*
*Purity reaches its perfection in the beardless boys,*
*But Vali, the beauty of the women is (even) greater!*

**Wali Muhammad Wali** (1667-1707), better known as Wali Gujarati. (Translation by Sunil Sharma; from Kulliyat-e Vali, edited by Nur al-Hasan Hashmi)

Top
*Bandhini print saree on the washing line*
Left
*In Surat, the saree-seller poses with pride*
*against the glitter and glamour of his wares*

The textile boom in the nineteenth century had seen women entering the workforce in a big way. Dalit and Vaghri women, especially, had worked alongside their men in the mills. In the 1920s, almost twenty percent of the workers were women.

What's even more interesting, since it was the mothers who introduced a woman into the workforce, many women took their mothers' names as surnames. This practice only changed in 1955, when husbands' or fathers' names began to be demanded by mill owners.

At the Information Office, you meet **Urmi** who advises: stay until Saturday. At 9 am, there is a new bus service, run by the corporation, which shows you everything there is to see in Surat. "All-Surat-tour."

As you turn to leave, Urmi surprises you with a compliment: 'Nice dress!' and with that, collapses into giggles.

"We are women. So of course, that's the first thing we notice. No?"

## Women!

Like **Gugiben** and **Gangaben**. Old women, giggling like teenaged girls, if you compliment them on their multiple tattoos. On their foreheads, on their necks, up their arms, down their legs, across their wrists, round their ankles, plunging down their chests. Tattooes, tattooes everywhere.

Peacocks, squares and circles, dots and lines, snakes, scorpions.

Their names. Their sisters' names and mothers-in-law's names and lovers' names.
**Inked into their bodies, forever.**

Top 1
*Saree bazaar, Surat - and naturally, women here again*

Top 2 and Left
*All the women from the tribes are exotically tattooed. They take it for granted - their lives imprinted on their skin; you are fascinated*

Left - Top
*Women everywhere, of all ages, here working on the thread looms in saree-city*

Left - Bottom
*Proudly she shows her tattoos, the Rabari woman from Zainabad*

**Varun** at the wholesale cloth shop will also tell you about 'masterminds'.

## "The man who can extract Rs 1000 from a rough diamond worth only Rs 100, that man is called a mastermind here."

These masterminds had to be imported, though. It was a Surati entrepreneur who brought home a boatload of diamond cutters from East Africa at the start of the last century. Today, India cuts anywhere between eighty to ninety percent of all diamonds. But that is in recent history. Once, India was the largest production centre for diamonds too.

In fact, it is believed that diamonds were first recognised as precious and mined in India. Thousands of years ago, the stone could actually be found along the river banks, wherever there was the right kind of alluvial soil. In ancient texts, there are references to the stone as the Sanskrit 'vajra' or thunderbolt. Perhaps, because the play of light in the polished stone reminded people of lightning and thunder. There are references to the value of diamonds in texts like the *Arthashastra*, written at some point between 350 and 283 BC. The text is one of the longest-surviving treatises from ancient India and was written by **Chanakya**, mentor and prime minister to the Mauryan king **Chandragupt** whose empire included much of modern Gujarat. While much of the text in *Arthashastra* deals with matters of policy, war and governance, Chanakya also wrote of the merits and demerits of diamonds. "Big, heavy, capable of bearing blows, with symmetrical points, capable of scratching a vessel, revolving like a spindle and brilliantly shining, is excellent. That (stone) with points lost, without edges and defective on one side, is bad."

At the heart of the multi-million dollar diamond business in India (or indeed, the world) lie two simple tenets: trust and integrity.

This glittering network – extending from Surat, and increasingly Navsari, in Gujarat to Mumbai and Antwerp – is only possible because of a cheap, reliable system of transportation. There is no security cover and, often, no soul-saving insurance either. All they have is people who honour the trust placed in them and who will, at considerable risk, transport both polished and unpolished diamonds for a small fee.

These people are the 'angadiyas', or couriers. While their claim to fame is the diamond business, traditionally, they have transported any precious merchandise, including expensive silk sarees, jewellery or other valuables.

The community is small in terms of numbers, but considering that nearly ninety percent of the stones in the international market are cut and polished in India, their significance can hardly be under-estimated.

While there have been a few reports of robberies, the angadiyas are usually able to deliver their cargoes successfully. Experts believe that this is possible only because the angadiyas are part of an intricate social network in which they know the right people; tough, powerful people who do not make for easy enemies.

While the diamond trade itself is new, as are the railways and flights, the system has existed for a few centuries. Angadiyas worked to make important deliveries across the subcontinent. They were a close-knit group of people, usually from the same caste, and unforgiving of betrayal.

Many of the couriers now work for registered angadiya firms, and some of the bigger ones handle diamonds and cash worth anywhere between one and five billion rupees everyday. The couriers themselves don't make even a tiny fraction of that.

Page 100-101
*The eye for the jewel. Say Surat and many will think Diamonds*

Top 1
*Searching for the heart of the gem*

Top 2
*Assembly lines of precise, expert work produces the best polished and sorted diamonds for the world*

Left - Top
*Diamond workers grinding the stones*

Left - Bottom
*Sorting the stones at a modern facility*

These are ordinary men, often not very highly educated, who take an overnight train between Mumbai and Surat. They are not armed or guarded and they carry their precious cargo – either diamonds or cash payments – in ordinary cloth bags or briefcases. Most of them have only their own watchful eyes to help them get through the journey safely. Many diamond merchants don't even take proper receipts that mention the size and value of the consignment. There is nothing to hold the system together barring a few chits of paper and a word of honour.

The Sardar Vallabhbhai Patel Museum in Surat appears to be a curious place, at first. All exhibits have succinct and basic labels: 'Vase', 'Jewellery', 'Copper vessels', 'Zalaramma', 'Burmese objects' and 'Wooden objects'. There is little information other than the obvious.

An eighteenth century 'Radha' (item 1202) is locked in place atop of a red box (item 4236), her arms missing, reminding you of the famous Venus de Milo. Next to her, stands 'Murlidhar' (item 1201), black as night, flowers in his ears, an arm and a hand missing. His flute is missing too.

The reason presents itself when the watchman tells you that the museum suffered a lot during the floods. There was 14 feet of water, he says. The whole city suffered, but the damage in this museum is almost irreparable.

The English cemetery is taken care of by **Bharatbhai**. He limps. Ever since his paralysis attack, some 12 years ago, he has been limping, and watching over this place. The limp does not prevent him from climbing up into tombs, two-storey high. He will insist that you climb up too – narrow and ancient though the stairs may be.

Amongst hundreds of others, lies buried Gerald Aungier, once President of Surat and Governor of Bombay. Died June 30th 1677. A very powerful man. Yet you need not spend much time here. The grave that really holds your interest belongs to a mere girl, who died on New Year's Eve, in the year that India fought its first war of independence.

On 31st Dec, 1857, aged 22, Catherine Theresa Allen died of consumption at Cambay. Somebody who loved her very dearly – Family? Friend? Lover? – let go of her with this:

> 'Translated by her God with spirit shriven
> She pass'd as t'were with smiles, from earth to heav'n
> Does youth, does beauty read the line?
> Does sympathetic fear their breast alarm?
> Speak, dear Kate! Breathe a strain divine
> E'en from the grave thou shalt have power to charm
> Bid them be chaste, as innocent as thee
> Bid them in duty's sphere as meekly move
> And if so fair, from vanity as free
> As firm in friendship, and as fond in love;
> Tell them though 'tis an awful thing to die
> ('twas e'en to thee) yet the dread path once trod
> Heaven lifts its everlasting portals high
> And bids the pure in heart, behold their God!
> Victorious o'er death, to her appear
> The vista'd joys of heaven's eternal year.'

Or, maybe, he never did let go.

Graves and gravestones are revealing, that way. They can sum up a life, a culture, or the history of a whole civilisation.

Take, for instance, the graves around the Mahabat Khan Makbara in Junagadh. Some of the older graves are marked entirely in Persian. Perhaps, dating to an age when Gujarati in its present form did not exist, or at least, the script was not often used. The later graves have markings

in both Persian and Gujarati. The ones who died after that have been bid farewell only in Gujarati.

In places such as the hilly, heavily-forested area to the south of the state, an area known as the Dangs, you might see painted or engraved stones. Often, these are found outside a tribal hamlet. These are called the '*palia*' or '*dev-palia*', variations of the totem pole. Here lies their history, their faith, their historic sense of courage.

*Mahuda* or the intoxicating *mahua* tree, *Limda* or the ever-useful *neem* tree, the sun, the moon. Peacocks, lions, the branch of a tree, to the creatures they lived with for centuries past: these are the images they want to take away along with their final breaths.

The *palia* are different for different communities. The Charans may have a rough representation of a man using a dagger on his own neck. The agriculturalists chose bullock carts. The sailors chose ships. The Rabaris – desert pastoralists – may show a figure riding a camel.

Each tribe put on its stone the things it knew, the things that defined a life that had ended.

There are many camels in sight. One stands contentedly near a bright yellow wall that advertises cement, in Sachin, a village not far from Surat. While the camel munches the sudden wealth of greens to his left and right, you have time to think about this village. Sachin was burnt down by the British in the aftermath of 1857.

But that was hardly the first time this region had suffered massive destruction. Before the British, it was the Marathas, led by Shivaji who had plundered Surat in 1664.

The Marathas had first wanted the merchants to negotiate a sizable ransom. When this was not done, the army sacked Surat and set hundreds of homes on fire. This was repeated in 1670. In fact, things got so bad that Surat would panic at the news of the Maratha army approaching. Merchants would quickly move out their goods and the harbour too suffered, for no ship wanted to dock there, with a sacking imminent. At the beginning of the eighteenth century, Surat was sacked for the third time, and slipped into a phase marked by torture, exploitation and corruption. Taxes were imposed even on marriage, and especially widow remarriage.

So much so, that when the British took over Surat, in 1759, there was widespread support amongst various groups including merchants, rulers of small kingdoms and social reformers – all for their own set of reasons. But by the time the first war of independence happened, in 1857, the picture was far from rosy.

Today, it is hard to imagine Surat as a bustling port. But it was once one of the most important ports and commercial hubs in the subcontinent, especially after Cambay began to decline, due to heavy silting. During the reign of the emperor Akbar, it was known as '*bandar-e-mubarak*': the blessed port. One of the many windows of the east to the west. In fact, the symbol of SUDA (Surat Urban Development Authority) is still an old-fashioned ship's anchor.

Climb up the old, wooden steps to the terrace, just above the office of the Conservator of Forests, and it is not so hard to imagine Surat as a once-bustling port town. From this creaky vantage point, where the sea stretches out as far as sea can stretch, you can stand, look out and imagine.

Surat Castle now houses The Court. It is also home to the Office of the Conservator of Forests and to the Police Record offices.

If you hang around on the terrace long enough, somebody like **Lakhabhai** might join you. He might ask, "You looking for old things? There are

Top
*Traditional bullock cart, still in use in the Dang habitats in the south*
Left - Top
*Children of the Dang tribe, straight-backed and earnest in school*
Left - Bottom
*Village art covers the huts, the homes of the Adivasi Dangs*

plenty of old things here. Many old criminal records!"

And he might slap you lightly on the arm and chuckle deeply.

Watch your step as you descend. There is moss on the stairs. And there is the clerk, **Waheeda Bano**'s easy smile, melting into the drizzle. Oh, the travel agent was so wrong.

**Aakar Patel**, former editor of Mid-Day and Divya Bhaskar, lives in Mumbai and describes himself as a Gujarati from Surat. He loves the music and dancing, especially during Navratri, the nine days of the festival that celebrate the Goddess Durga, which is full of fun and the energy of community dancing. He likes the urbanity, the mercantile culture, which is inclusive and pragmatic, and does away with 'notions of honour', as evidenced by Gujarati women who seem visibly more empowered than many other Indian communities. He is very fond of Surati food, especially '*Bhusu, Ghari, Undhiyu, Tapela nu Mutton*, the snacky stuff'.

However, he is a dyed-in-the-er...textile 'Surati', who isn't that fond of Ahmedabad. He says, "Surat is also fond of open trade, but it has an inclusive culture that is closer to Mumbai's than to Gujarat's."

Amongst other things, he loves the food stalls in Surat. "The Khatris stand behind the best food stalls in Surat, if you're non-vegetarian. Their women sit, and drink with the men at social functions, unique among Gujaratis and perhaps among Indians. I do not mean to say that meat and drink are the hallmark of an open society. But in India, where the notion of pollution is socially strong, they are a good indicator."

Top
*The Gujarati sweet tooth craves more. Mohan Mithai, Surat*

Left
*Bring the world to Surat! Eiffel Chowk has a brightly lit replica of the real thing*

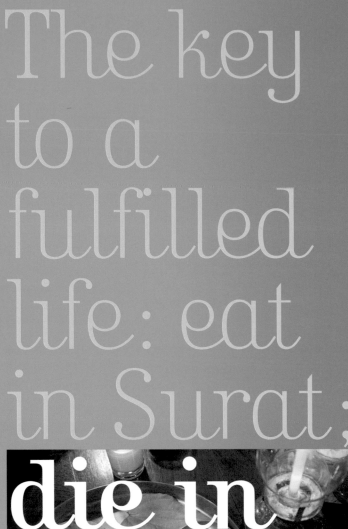

The key to a fulfilled life : eat in Surat; **die in Kashi.**

# Food, Fulfillment

सुरत नું જમણ અને કાશી નું મરણ
*Surat nu jaman ane kashi nu maran!*

**Ask any Gujarati** – what is dearest to his/her heart, and food is right up there, topping the list.

Not surprising, considering the sheer variety and the scale of teasers available to the slurping palate. There is a sixteenth century text, *Varnak-samuchchaya*, which lists about nine hundred types of foods. This includes thirty-six types of *laddoos*, and items such as *dhokla, khandvi* and *idli* (also described as idari or idada). By this century, Persian items too had made their way into the list – *badam, khadbuj, jardalu*. There was *narangi* and there was *halwa*.

Much of contemporary Gujarati cuisine is a reminder of Gujaratis' frequent travel needs. Forever on the move, the trader-traveller (or more correctly, his wife) responded by tucking into loads of pickles, chutneys and dry 'snacks' that wouldn't rot.

Even today, in large parts of Gujarat, people's bellies have a soft spot for *bajra* and *jowar* rather than wheat, a preference that harks back all the way to the Indus Valley Civilisation, as does the use of sesame and linseed oil for cooking.

**Sheetal Lakhia**: Businessman. Silk weaver. Die-hard foodie.

This is the man who has, quite literally, covered the country from Kashmir to Kanyakumari. North to south and from east to west and far abroad. All for the love of the palate.

Sheetal Lakhia takes his food seriously. He travels to eat. Lakhia knows the nooks and crannies of cities through their cuisine and he maintains a library full of books and films about food. When he talks about cuisine, you listen.

"Gujarati food changes every hundred and fifty kilometres. The basic dish remains the same, the taste will change. The daal at Limdi is different from the daal in Ahmedabad, different in Bharuch and Surat."

"Ahmedabad was a city built by a Muslim ruler and has a great legacy of excellent non-vegetarian food. Also, since many of the families in Gujarat stayed back during partition, their gastronomic legacy is still alive here."

"For non-vegetarian food.... Well, there is the fried chicken... oh, that fried chicken! It is like.... like, like *sheera*. There is so much ghee that you have to just scoop it up and eat it. You cannot tear at it or break off chunks. The best place to go for such fried chicken is Bhatiyaar Gali."

"Roti Gali in Ahmedabad is one place worth going to just for the fantastic view. You see large, round, baked *naans*, like loaves of bread strung up for display. And there are huge, sweet, *farmaishi naans* for special occasions. The best place is Hussain Bakery in Teen Darwaza. The man behind the counter will get it out of the oven and hand it to you, balanced on his fingertips. He cannot hold the naan by one edge, because it will fall apart – it is that rich."

"*Haleem* – it is like *khichda* and you get it in both sweet and salty versions. It is a Gujarati Bohri specialty but the only place you get authentic Haleem

There are many false images and identities of Gujarat. For instance, this thing about vegetarian food. Gujarat has many, many communities that eat a lot of non-vegetarian food.

Gujarat is also one of those places where the Muslims came first as traders and only later as rulers. You find signs of the difference in Sidhpur, which was the capital of Sidhraj Solanki. In that region, many had converted to Islam and even now, we find Muslims there who have legal traditions, which are not derived from the Prophet Muhammad's strictures. The systems of property and inheritance and divorce are somewhat different. In fact, many converted Muslims still carry their Brahmanical Gotra names while many are vegetarian.

**Arvind Shah,** sociologist.

Title inset
*Eggs cooked in different ways. Some of the roadside stalls only open for business after 12 at night*

Top 1
*Dabeli, a new variation on bread buns filled with spicy potato and pomegranate filling*

Top 2
*Khari-sing, peanuts roasted in salt*

Left
*Visions of fulfillment : the dhokla, synonymous with Gujarat; a tempting thali at the upmarket Agasher restaurant; channa chor garam, endless savouries - everywhere the food calls out to you and you stop to eat*

is Ahmedabad. It is basically broken wheat, soaked in milk for a couple of days. Then, the spices and meat are added, with a final garnishing of fried onions. For more everyday Bohra food, go to the Bohra cemetery near Kalupur. There are a couple of small eateries that serve the very excellent staple: *daal-chawal-palaida*."

"Amongst non-vegetarian dishes, an interesting one is *Kaachu*. The Koli community used to make it. Raw meat, marinated for eight to nine days – that's *kaachu*. It tastes so soft and so tender. It is just unbelievable."

"As for the Gujarati Thali – it used to be a wholesome and healthy affair but it has changed beyond recognition over the years. Now it has become very high-funda; you can get it in a range from Rs 35 to Rs 400, depending on what's in it. And dessert? Gujarati cuisine doesn't really have the concept of 'dessert'. Sweets are served along with the rest of the food – such as *basundi, doodh-pak, aam ras, sheera*."

One of the most delicious yes, delicious, spots in Ahmedabad is the HBM House, now a heritage hotel. While it does have a pretty terrace restaurant – Agashiye – the deliciousness associated with it is not merely gastronomic. Its very name is a succulent bit of local history.

HBM stands for Hun, Bawo ane Mangaldas. That is, 'Me, the Parsi and Mangaldas'.

'Hun' stood for Isaji Soma, a Muslim businessman. Bawa, local slang for Parsi men, stood for Homi Mehta, one of the partners and Mangaldas was the one who built this converted haveli: Mangaldas Girdhardas. This team of businessmen forged a very successful alliance and set up several ventures together. Their partnership was the stuff of legends in Ahmedabad; it is said that they were so well-known that any new successful business venture was assumed to be their doing.

| એન્ડ | સ્વ.શેઠ શ્રી નટવરલાલ માણેકલાલ સોની | | |
|---|---|---|---|
| ખણામાં<br>ાવ રૂ. | **Item** | **Rates in Oil** | **Rates in Butter** |
| ૪૦ | Regular Bhaji | 30 | 40 |
| ૩૫ | Only Bhaji | 25 | 35 |
| ૨૫ | Half Plate Bhaji / Pulav | 20 | 25 |
| ૪૫ | Sp. Bhaji Pav | 35 | 45 |
| ૪૫ | Boiled Bhaji | 35 | 45 |
| ૫૦ | Sp. Cheez Boiled Bhaji | 40 | 50 |
| ૫૫ | Kaju Drax Bhaji | 45 | 55 |
| ૪૫ | Sp. Green Bhaji | 35 | 45 |
| ૪૦ | Jain Bhaji | 33 | 40 |
| ૪૦ | Potato Cancelled Bhaji | 33 | 40 |
| ૪૦ | Tomato Cancelled Bhaji | 33 | 40 |
| ૪૦ | Pease Cancelled Bhaji | 33 | 40 |
| ૩૦ | Masala Pav with Bhaji | 25 | 30 |
| ૮ | Extra Bread | 6 | 8 |
| ૧૫ | (Garlic) Lassan-ni Chatni | 15 | 15 |
| ૭ | Onion Fry | 6 | 7 |
| -- | Papad Roasted | 3 | -- |
| -- | Fry Papad | 6 | -- |
| -- | Butter mili | 5 | -- |
| | **Pulav** | | |
| ૪૦ | Regular Veg. Pulav | 32 | 40 |

*The Gujarati attitude to food is reflected in our travel. We don't like to experiment very much. That's why so much of our food is dry – so that it may last. Dishes like Khakhra were invented when merchants, especially from Kutch, began to sail abroad, especially to Africa for the slave trade.*

*You will notice now, all the major airlines now offer a Jain option on the menu. In fact, recently, Air France had run an ad campaign in Gujarat with hoardings advertising 'Paris ma patra'... Now, that is typically Gujarati. We want to go to Paris but we want to eat our own food there. We will go to Ladakh and order a Gujarati Thali. The average Gujarati cannot stand more than twenty-four hours of non-Gujju food. That's why, many people carry their snacks with them even on planes, despite knowing they will get veg food there.*

*And yet, little innovations happen within the mould. Women are doing very well as entrepreneurs in the food sector. Ulhasben makes instant khichdi mix and other instant mixes of all the popular Gujarati dishes, which are sold the world over. Induben Khakhrawala has popularised not only conventional variations of khakhra like masala or methi, but also spring-roll khakhra and sweet-n-sour Chinese flavour khakhra!*

**Sheetal Lakhia**, die-hard foodie

Left
*Amazing what you can do with Bhaji!*
*A must-read Pav Menu at a food stall;*
*Manek Chowk, Ahmedabad*
Top
*Bhajiyas, battered deep fried vegetables*
Far Left
*Frying a perfect shoal of Pomfret*

Top and Left
*Saunfs and spices. The flavour of 'Gujju' cuisine comes from a delicate mix of ingredients, used individually and together. Shops pile these attractively, there will be many customers - Gujaratis love their own native cuisine the most and all cooks and housewives cater to refined tastes*

# Like Sugar in Milk

**The leaves glint.** Banana plantations. Coconut palms. Banyan trees.

Along this stretch, from Navsari to Udwada, you see glimpses of heaven. You can see why the Parsis chose to settle here, why they did not move headquarters to a city like Bombay or Surat. Who would?

If you like stories, go visit **Merwanji P Dastur** at Udwada. One of the oldest residents, the former priest will lean back into his rocking chair, and begin at the very beginning.

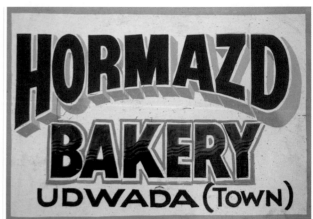

"Our fire is 1282 years old. We brought it with us when we ran from Iran, in 697 AD. We ran for our dharma. We took our kids and our fire and our oracle and we set sail. The west, we were convinced, would destroy our faith, so we came to Hindustan. We reached Diu and spent 19 years there. Then we set out again in our little vessel. But there was a cyclone and we began to pray that if we survive, we would build a big fire temple. Well, we survived, and landed at Sanjan Bandar. That was ruled by King Jadirana. We came as refugees but we were from a warrior nation. When we sought permission to stay, the King sent a full glass of milk and our leader understood the hidden message. He returned it full, and sweet."

This coded exchange of messages through a glass of milk is a famous story that almost each child in Gujarat knows. When the king sent a glass that was full to the brim, he meant to send out the message that there was no more room in the kingdom to accommodate outsiders. The Parsi leader understood this, so he carefully mixed sugar into the

*Title inset*
*Inside an Irani bakery; wherever there are Parsis you will find the irresistable Irani bakery*

*Top*
*Once again, the bakery. Hormazd is a popular bakery in Udwada*

*Left*
*Smile like honey; a little Parsi boy all dressed up for a celebratory occasion*

glass without spilling any milk and sent it back to the king. The king tasted the milk and understood the message: the Parsis would blend in with the locals as easily as sugar does in milk, and the citizens of the kingdom would not suffer on their account. The king gave the Parsis permission to stay, and they have stayed on ever since.

In the telling, Dastur always uses the first person plural. As if he himself had been there, seen it all, he describes their petition, to be allowed to build a fire temple, which was granted.

"In Hindustan, you can practice your faith. We asked, and the king said, *Koi vaanda nahin!*"

> "We spent more than three hundred years in Sanjan. But our *marafiz* predicted that we would face an attack, so we retreated to mountains. For 12 years, we hid in the mountains near Barot, with our fire. Luckily we found a stream nearby. Even now, we go up to the mountains sometimes. To pray. We see that even the local tribals light lamps at the spot where the fire had been kept."

The conflict, finally, come from within the community. Dastur narrates this with a sparkling twinkle in his eye.

"After three-four hundred years, in Navsari, there was a fight in the priestly council. We went to court and the king said, the holy fire should be divided into half, to satisfy both rival factions. We said, no. And one day, when the opposition went on family picnic, we took a chance. We stole the fire and left Navsari. After a few years, wandering around Valsad, we came here to Udwada, which was earlier 'oontwada'. We kept rebuilding our temple. Motibhai Wadia built this one."

"I used to be a priest. One of the old managers. Now I am 81 years old. There were nine families here in Udwada, and even now, each takes turns for the *kriya* and other duties at the temple."

Dastur himself had moved to Zanzibar in Africa, to work in an *agiari* but after eighteen years, he was forced to return because of a violent revolution. "We weren't welcome any longer. I tried working in Bombay later, but didn't like the fast life. Came back here, where my dad was a farmer. Stayed a bachelor..."

He trails off, and begins to look into the distance. The beautiful distance of emerald horizons.

"I worry about the sea. It rises. They build walls. But the sea ... you can't stop the sea."

Navsari. One of the oldest cities in Gujarat with a history spanning 2000 years, with a mention in ancient Greek writings, a city that witnessed many rulers and reigns, right up to the Gaekwads of Baroda before India's independence. 17 kms away is Dandi, famous for the Dandi march where Mahatma Gandhi and his followers protested against the British salt tax.

Top 1
*The details on the walls inside Parsi homes in Udwada; an old clock*

Top 2
*Ahura Mazda, the wise Lord of the Zorastrians, protects and is honoured in the homes of the devout Parsis*

Left - Top
*Dastur, a Parsi priest*

Left - Bottom
*BN Seervai Parsi Dharamshala*

Navsari. Home to the sacred fire of the Parsis for nearly four hundred years. Buildings reflecting Parsi architecture can be seen in the city, an oft-visited one, being the Parsi Vad which is now a heritage site. Even today, Navsari is known as the 'headquarters' of the community that gave us leaders such as Jamsetji Tata and Dadabhoy Naoroji. The latter was known as the Grand Old Man of India, our earliest nationalist politician.

**Dr. Dadabhoy Naoroji** was born in Navsari in 1825 into a family that was far from wealthy. His father died when he was a child and his mother struggled to put him through school and college. However, Dadabhoy was always a brilliant student and won several scholarships. He was especially good at Mathematics and would have been sent to study in England right after school, if it had not been for his circumstances and the turbulence of the first war of independence. As things were, he had to take up a job instead but he did go to England eventually. He also helped found the Indian National Congress here.

Dadabhoy Naoroji spent many years of his life in London, where he had formed an East India Association. Almost every Indian who went there to study went to him first with letters of introduction, including Jinnah and Gandhi.

In 1892, he was elected a member of the British Parliament (with a young and admiring Mohammed Ali Jinnah serving as his campaign assistant); he was the first Indian parliamentarian and proved that he was both able and worthy, doing his utmost to argue India's cause with her rulers.

**Jamsetji Tata** was one of the few Indian industrialists of his era who did not like the ruling British; the sentiment was mutual for they did not shower him with honours such as a knighthood.

Jamsetji was one of the pioneers of the textile revolution that led to Ahmedabad being called the Manchester of the East. However, Tata chose to set up a cloth mill in Nagpur, instead of Mumbai or Ahmedabad, since he wanted it to be somewhere closer to the fields where cotton was grown. And, though he did not live to see his dreams become tangible, but the country's first iron and steel plant and a hydroelectric plant were very much the result of his efforts.

We also owe him the Tata Institute of Fundamental Research and, of course, India's first 'native' luxury hotel, the Taj Mahal Hotel in Mumbai. It is a well-known legend by now – the story of how Jamsetji was refused entry into a hotel, since he was an Indian. He responded by building that glorious thing by the sea. Even today – despite the glut of five-and-seven-star hotels dotting our metropolitan cities – tourists like to take boat rides a short distance from the Gateway of India, so they can look at the magnificent contours of the Taj Hotel against the sunset.

However, industry and business alone would not have made Jamsetji the giant he was. That really can only be attributed to his empathy for the common man and the poor, and his sense of justice. He did not wait for laws to insist on provident funds and clean, decent working conditions for his workers. And he made sure that even after he was gone, much of his money went into trusts that continue to fund that empathy.

*We do not ask any favours. We want only justice.*
**Dadabhoy Naoroji,** the Grand Old Man of India, in 1906.

Top
*The grand old man, Dadabhoy Naoroji; a statue in Navsari*

Left
*Different perspectives of the Maharaja of Vansda's Palace built in 1913. Here again, the Palace is today home to just one man*

# Honestly Headstrong

**Another well-known** person who was born in Navsari is **Ketan Mehta**.

His film career has been a very checkered one; he went from making *Mirch Masala* to *Maya Memsaab* to *The Rising* (better known simply as *Mangal Pandey*), to *Sardar*, a biopic on the life of **Sardar Vallabhbhai Patel**, one of the best-known and best-loved politicians of Gujarat.

Born Vallabhbhai Jhaverbhai Patel into a farmer family in Nadiad, he worked hard to educate himself and gradually ended up in the legal profession. Starting from the district court at Godhra, he went on to England to study law and returned to set up a practice in Ahmedabad. Before he threw himself full-time into the freedom struggle, he had quite a firm reputation as a criminal lawyer. From there to politics was one short step. By 1918, he was involved with a farmers' protest that is remembered as the *Kheda Satyagrah*. He was also municipal councillor for Ahmedabad during the 1920s – a difficult time, since the city was confronted with plagues, famines and floods.

Sardar Patel was already working alongside Mahatma Gandhi and the other leaders of the freedom movement. India's 'nightingale', freedom-fighter and poet, Sarojini Naidu had taken the liberty of calling him '*Bardoli ka bail*' (the bull from Bardoli). He was also known as the 'Iron Man' (partly because of his steely determination to finish what he set his mind to, and partly because of his impatience with emotion) and he was one of the first leaders of stature to agree to the partition proposal put forward by the British and he is believed to have eventually prevailed upon Gandhi, Nehru and others to give their assent. He had not foreseen the tragedies that Partition would bring, perhaps.

Sardar Patel's real work started after Independence.

In 1948, as Deputy Prime Minister of India, Sardar Vallabhbhai Patel undertook the most unenviable task of all and it surely must have demanded all his powers of persuasion, aggression, diplomacy and tenacity. He had to get about 565 Rajas and Nawabs to give up their independent states and accede to the Union of India.

For the most part, he succeeded. Some rulers, like Bhavnagar and Baroda, came willingly. Hyderabad was forced to accede through the use of the army. Kashmir continues to burn.

Title inset
*In memory of a patriot*

Top
*The Sardar Vallabhbhai Patel Museum
Shahibaug, Ahmedabad*

Left
*Sardar Vallabhbhai Patel and Gandhiji; a
history of struggle, resolve and independence*

At **Sabarmati Ashram**, a group of school girls sit cross-legged on the floor, singing *'pyaasa hiran jaise dhoonde hai jal ko'* and a group of boys runs about the corridors. They are drenched with the constant rain and their own constant laughter.

They ask to be photographed.

You ask them their names.

Sunil, Sumit, Vijay, Rakesh, Gautam. They all live in Juno Vadaj and Nava Vadaj. They come here in the evenings. Their Papa-Mummy sent them here – "to say namaste to Gandhiji".

"Because he lived here."

You talk about Gandhiji. They giggle and ask for a photograph. They don't know if he is alive, or when he died or how.

**"Who killed Gandhi?"**

"Who? Mathu - ? Who is Nathuram Godse?"

**"The British must have killed him."**

"What do you mean 'our own people'? Must have been 'your' people; couldn't be ours."

"Where are you from? **Did the UP-wale kill Gandhiji?"**

"Let me find the one who killed Gandhi. I'll shoot him."

"Hudd! Don't be mad."

# Swadesh:
## Our Own Land

**Gujarat is the** 'native place' of several of the foremost politicians and nationalists of the last century.

### After all, the fathers of both nations – India and Pakistan – belonged to Gujarat and their mother tongue was Gujarati.

Apart from Dadabhoy Naoroji, Gandhi and Jinnah, there was Badruddin Tyabji, Pherozeshah Mehta, Vallabhbhai Patel and Rahimtullah M Sayani. Interestingly, many of the leaders of the freedom struggle came from trader families, and many of them were trained lawyers themselves. Since traders owned mills and factories, they were enthusiastic supporters of Gandhiji's call for Swadeshi.

The Swadeshi movement helped us win our freedom, we are told. We are told about khadi and hand-made sandals. What we are not told is that it helped us create heavenly delights such as the *naankhatai*.

*Naankhatai* is one of the few indigenous biscuits you'll ever taste, and it came to be so popular thanks to the Swadeshi movement. When the call was given to boycott all British goods, imported biscuits had to go flying out of the window. Parsi bakers in Surat responded by baking hard flour with ghee. The result was the naankhatai, which was quickly added on the menu of all the local tea-shops, across Gujarat and Bombay.

Leaders of the Swadeshi movement also came from merchant families. Actually, traders have always had a huge say in Gujarati politics. Even in ancient times, it was the traders who held important ministerial positions. Sample this statement, made by one of the most powerful ministers in Patan, Vastupal.

### "I am a vanik, well-known in the shop of battlefield. I buy commodities, the head of enemies...and pay the price in the form of heaven."

**Vastupal** (in response to a provocation from the ruler of Lat.)

**Sabarmati**, at the fringes of Ahmedabad city and situated on the banks of the Sabarmati River, is home to the famous Sabarmati Ashram, the hub from where Mahatma Gandhi set up home and started the Dandi March. Also called Satyagraha Ashram during the independence movement, this is a calm and peaceful place, with shady trees and has a museum and a library with details from the life of Gandhi including letters, manuscripts, films and books. The Ashram also has photo galleries and an auditorium. There is a myth surrounding the site. The sage, Dadhichi Rishi, was believed to have donated his bones for a righteous war, and Gandhi believed it was the right place to carry out satyagraha activities.

---

**Naankhatai recipe.**

1 cup maida
1 tsp baking powder
1/4 tsp vanilla essence
1/2 cup ghee
1/2 cup sugar
2 tsps chopped cashews (optional)
1 tsp elaichi powder

Seive flour and baking powder together. Add vanilla essence. Mix ghee and sugar separately till the paste is smooth. Add the flour and the elaichi (cardamom) powder. Knead properly and divide this mixture into equal-sized balls. Press these into a round, flat shape, and place them upon a greased baking tray. Put in the oven (heated at 375 degrees) for about 20-25 minutes.

Take out of the oven (wear gloves) and breathe deep. Yes, that is one of the scents of heaven.

*I would not be deserving of that freedom if I did not cherish and treasure the equal right of every other race, weak or strong, to the same freedom.*

Mohandas Karamchand Gandhi

Title inset
*Celebrating the common man. Much of Gujarat's art and sculpture honours the people of the land - the farmers, the workers, the craftsmen*
Left
*Children playing in front of a statue in Surat*

# Tales From Now, and Long Ago

**'Sardar'**, Ketan Mehta's film, received due recognition when it was honoured with the Nargis Dutt Award for the best feature film on national integration. However, the film that first brought Mehta the most critical acclaim, and perhaps the one that was hardest to make, was his debut film *'Bhavni Bhavai'*. It falls back upon a dramatic folk form and just like the intent of the theatrical original, it is a work of art rooted in protest. The film, made in Gujarati, is dedicated to Asait Thakore, who is generally known as the father of *Bhavai*.

**Asait Thakore** probably did not invent the dramatic form but he did write many of the plays that were performed by later generations. *Bhavai* was a folk performance intricately linked to the oppression of lower castes and classes. The story of how Thakore, a Brahmin, came to be associated with this form is also a fascinating legend.

It is believed that Thakore was a priest from Sidhpur in the fourteenth century. A local farmer's daughter was carried away by a Subedaar. Thakore went to bring her back and, perhaps in an attempt to lend more weight to his argument, told the Subedaar that she was his own daughter. The latter did not believe him, so he asked the priest to eat off the same plate to prove that she was indeed his daughter. Usually, Brahmins would not share a plate with someone from a lower caste. Thakore decided to cast away his caste taboo and ate off the same plate. He brought the girl back but when he returned, he found himself boycotted by his own caste. When he was excommunicated, he went to live with the lower caste communities.

From this point on, the Brahmin began to write poems and plays which were performed in the folk form we know as *bhavai*. He may have written as many as three hundred of these plays although only sixty of the texts have survived. Full of satire and ringing with a bitter indictment of the caste orthodoxy, while infused with dramatic energy, these texts are testaments to the lives of the ordinary – the cobblers and farmers, nomads and thieves, sadhus and fakirs – their loves and betrayals, myths and jests.

Over the years, *bhavai* has evolved in ways that offer a clue to the evolution of the culture of the region. It uses a mixture of Gujarati, Marwari, Urdu and Hindi. The instruments include the *pakhwaj* and *sarangi* as well as a long copper pipe called *Bhungi* while the musical form is a mixture of Hindustani and folk traditions.

As much as it is a form of self-expression and an art-form, it is also an offering to the Gods. Or the mother-goddess, to be precise. At Ambaji, one of the fifty-one Shakti peeths, *bhavai* performances are very much a part of the navratri celebrations.

> *"Morning*
> *A beauty, this island city, draped in veils*
> *Asleep and dreaming on the ocean's waves,*
> *Death's mask on her face, song's surma in her eye;*
> *Diamonds glitter on her gently heaving bosom.*
>
> *The unclaimed corpse of peace lies on the roads,*
> *no stink from this; only street-lamps shudder,*
> *and shutting eyes, put out their lights.*

"**Impossible** is he to be attained by yajna, yoga, meditation and austerities

Hard to have sight of, even in dreams,

Yet see how Hari is attained by **love!**"

*Curious, the sun, peers over the horizon*
*(any excuse to rise is good enough!)*
*his head splits open, its blood spills out,*
*the whole sky blazes then with reddish light."*

(Extracted from *Gayatri*, in 'Coral Island', a collection of poetry by **Niranjan Bhagat**, translated by Suguna Ramanathan and Rita Kothari.)

શબ્દ–અવતાર
પૂર્ણમાંથી અંશ અવતારી થયો,
સ્વાદ કાજે શબ્દ સંસારી થયો.
'તું' થઇને શુદ્ધ શૃંગારી થયો,
'હું' થઈ અવધૂત અલગારી થયો.
કંદરા એ, કાળ એ, ગોરંભ એ,
મૌન એ, ને એજ ઉદ્ગારી થયો.
મુક્ત સ્વેચ્છાએ જ બંધાયો સ્વમાં,
સ્થિર મટીને કેવો સંચારી થયો !
તેજ, માટી, મૂર્તિ, મંદિર, આરતી,
એ જ પુષ્પો થઇને પૂજારી થયો !

Rajendra Shukla
27 January 1978
Gazal Sanhita, Mandal 1 p. 11

**Rajendra Shukla**, poet, recipient of the Narsinh Mehta award, the highest for Gujarati poets, is one of the best-known ghazal writers in Gujarati.

"For the last thirty-five or forty years, I've been specialising in the Gujarati ghazal. Earlier, it was a second-class citizen in the regional literature, but now it is an accepted part of the mainstream. You see ghazals in text books too."

"The Ghazal came from Persian and developed in Urdu, but simultaneously, Gujarati also adopted the poetic form. But the content of the Gujarati ghazal is unique. The metaphors and symbols used have changed. Originally, 'jaam' (the cup) and 'saaki' (the wine-bearer) used to represent divine ecstasy. I've introduced 'kartal', the instrument that sadhus play when they get *mast*. You see, Oriental poetry tends to be epigrammatic. However long, an epic will have complete couplets, just like a ghazal. Harmony, balance and aesthetics – that is the essence of innovations in *chhand-shastra*. Traditionally, we used the Vedic metre. In the '60s, the modern influence was felt in language too. The metre went from the Persian traditional to a different Gujarati metre. This was significant because the natural cadence of a language decides the poetic metre. Later poets have used their own metre. I used the Jaichand metre."

"Rhyme is important more in Persian poetry. In Sanskrit, the rhyme is not important. The modern languages (like Urdu and Gujarati) are flexible. You can use two short vowels instead of one long one. Urdu made this possible and Gujarati changed in both ways, to develop the ghazal."

"Since I am also a Sanskrit and Apabrahmsh scholar, I turned to spiritualism early. The purpose of poetry is to know yourself. Let ego melt and the reader be drawn in. The word is my way of finding myself. The medieval poets were a strong influence."

"Gujarati poets mostly focus on self-expression. They are not contemporary in their content. In that sense, not 'poets of their times'. Their social and political consciousness is less. But then, the modern poets are less gross, more subtle. More introspective. Society is more interested in itself. The piercing nature of poetry is gone. So, self-expression alone is enough. There are no 'isms' attached. Poetry is not a tool for change, here."

"At fourteen, I knew my destiny was to become a poet. I also decided not to write anything until I turned twenty. The ghazal is a constrained form and the challenge is to say the most with the least possible use of words. So, it appealed to me. It is also similar to the *shlok*, the *doha* and so on. Besides, I also read a lot of Wali Gujarati, growing up in Junagadh."

Left - Top
*Priest practising yoga at Kalo Dungar temple*
Left - Bottom
*Extracted from 'Celebration of Divinity', a collection of Bhakti poems by Narsinh Mehta, the father of Gujarati poetry, and translated by Darshana Trivedi and Rupalee Burke*

# Men, Mavericks, Moving Images

**Lately, Gandhi** has re-entered our lives. And, while his message remains the same, the medium is different – through theatre and film, we are being reintroduced to the man this nation calls Bapu.

What we didn't know about the Mahatma as a man, a father, **Feroze Abbas Khan** is telling us through *'Gandhi, My Father'*.

The story of how he got around to making the film is also interesting. Khan has been a well-known theatre personality in Mumbai, and he first made *'Gandhi Vs Gandhi'* as a theatre production that has been staged successfully for years, before it was adapted for the screen. Though not a Gujarati himself, Khan had grown up with Gujarati neighbours, and not only did he pick up the language, he actually got involved with Gujarati theatre, thanks to the years spent in NMC (Narsee Monjee College in Mumbai).

In addition to that, he ended up marrying a Gujarati woman and his father-in-law lives in Ahmedabad. The culture, now, is very much a part of his being.

He says that the film was actually shot in Gujarat. "We could have built a set but when we saw the way Harilal's house (in Ahmedabad) has been preserved, with a lot of the old atmosphere still intact even in the surroundings, we decided to shoot in the original location. That whole stretch is very well-preserved and still looks like the houses from those times (sixty years ago) would have looked."

Some of his fondest working memories include the time spent shooting at Sarkhej Roza. "We were treated so warmly by the people. We would be shooting late at night and people would bring cups of tea. When the light-man would get tired, they'd even help to hold the lights. We needed total silence around, not even the hum of the air-conditioners, so they switched them off willingly."

The other Gujarati theatre veteran who moved successfully to Hindi films is **Vipul Shah**, also a product of NM College, and married, as it happens, to Shefali, the actress who played Kasturba, in *'Gandhi, My Father'*.

Shah is credited with making one of the most original films in recent Bollywood history: *'Ankhen'*, the story of three blind men pulling off a bank robbery. The film was based on the play *'Aandhado Pato'*, which also had a very successful stage stint before the screen version.

A proud Kutchi who returns often to the spectacular desert that is his homeland, Shah has also had a successful stint in the television world. Actually, if there is the curious overbearance of Gujarati family intrigue on Indian television – almost all of the soaps have business families as their main protagonist and intra-family conflict as the central theme – you have Vipul Shah to blame.

He admits to the charge too, laughing. "Well, you could say that I am to blame, partly. After working for a while in TV, we made the Hindi serial *'Ek Mahal Ho Sapno Ka'*, based on a Gujarati joint family, and *'Alpaviram'*, which was adapted from a Gujarati novel, on Sony TV. *Ek Mahal...* which was about the ordinary events in the lives of a joint family became very popular, and was one of the first shows in India to complete a thousand episodes. The others have followed the pattern."

Title inset
*Collage of a poster of Feroz Abbas Khan's film Gandhi - My Father*

Top
*Sarkhej Roza, Ahmedabad*

Left - Top
*The movie poster maker; it is a dwindling tribe, fewer Gujarati films, digital posters; but he still has work and continues to earn a living as a cog in the big wheel of entertainment*

Left - Bottom
*The Prince Cinema in Vadodara, showing a Gujarati film. Many of the larger towns now have spiffy new movie halls, some old ones like these still survive*

Since Vipul's first soap that had a Gujarati family as its protagonist, there have been other television serials that have had similar backdrops, such as the impossibly long-running but still hugely popular 'Kyunki Saas Bhi Kabhi Bahu Thi'. Newer ones include 'Teen Bahuraniyan', 'Ghar Ki Lakshmi... Betiyaan', 'Aati Rahengi Baharein' and comedy shows like 'Baa, Bahu aur Baby' and 'Khichdi'.

For the rest of the Hindi soap story, reach for the remote. Saas-bahu, Tulsi-Ba, Ba-Baby et al, show no signs of throwing in the towel just yet.

Many of the successful Gujarati names in Indian television today have made their way to the small screen via the stage.

They have done well in that city of dreams, Mumbai, which is not surprising considering that nearly twenty-five percent of the population there is of Gujarati origin. In fact, it is said that as far as Gujarati theatre is concerned, Mumbai is its capital city.

The story of Gujarati plays on the stage dates back to 1853, with the opening show of a play called 'Rustom, Jabuli and Sorab'. This was probably a typical production of what has been described as 'Parsi theatre'. While there had been a long tradition of performances such as bhavai, the folk format was not designed as a stage production and was not very popular in urban centres. Until then, Gujarati theatre did not have the scripts that would give it a distinct, modern identity. With Parsi theatre, that changed, and over the next hundred and fifty odd years, Gujarati plays became increasingly popular amongst entertainment-seekers in the cities.

When Gujarat was still a part of the 'Bombay' state, the newly formed theatre groups benefitted from the support of the Bharatiya Vidya Bhavan and the contests organised by the state government. It was during this phase, in the 1950s, that the respected names from the Gujarati stage made their breakthrough appearances.

In the seventies, there was a fresh influx of talent from a generation that included **Mahendra Joshi**, **Paresh Rawal**, **Homi Wadia**, **Sujata Mehta** and **Daisy Rani**, many of whom went on to work in films.

Just as most of the talent grows in, or moves to, Mumbai, it also comes back from that city. Many performances are staged by touring troupes based in Mumbai, although there are a fair number of troupes based in both Ahmedabad and Vadodara.

However, not everybody is pleased with the state of affairs with reference to theatre. Critics are upset about the lack of sensitivity and of probing voices and a slide into comfort zones. One of the most prolific, and most dedicated critics is **Utpal Bhayani**. A chartered accountant with a passion for theatre, he has reviewed over five hundred plays through a column he writes for the Janbhoomi-Pravasi based in Mumbai.

His reviews have been collected and published as four volumes: Drishya-falak, Preksha, Tarjanisanket and Sanga-bhoomi. According to Bhayani, the very thing that made the success of these new productions possible – the audiences need for fun on a weekend – has been their undoing as well. Nevertheless, for an audience that is looking for fun – boisterous, musical, naughty or otherwise – there is no dearth of productions. And, for subtlety and candour, there are critics like Utpal Bhayani.

One of the nascent Gujarati names in Indian television is that of **Jamnadas Majethia**, a product of the Mudra Institute who trained in advertising to begin with, but moved to theatre and TV very quickly. Today, he heads 'Hats Off Productions' along with partner **Aatish Kapadia**, which is responsible for popular sitcoms like 'Khichdi', 'Sarabhai Vs Sarabhai' and 'Batliwala House No. 43'.

Majethia had admitted in interviews that he started off wanting to be an actor. When those plans didn't go anywhere, he switched over to Gujarati

theatre. He also switched from acting to production, and he had a clutch of very successful plays in Mumbai, and from dramatics to television was but a few short steps.

His latest show, 'Batliwala's House No. 43' morphed into a more hilarious 'Kudkudiya House No. 43'. The eccentric Parsi family was replaced by orthodox, loud Gujaratis, who also run a *farsaan* shop in the house and the whole team appears to be doing very well with television audiences.

There's more to entertainment than TV, of course, and there's more to film than Bollywood, as there should be. While there is a small bunch of men and women committed to independent films and documentary work, Gujarati films are floundering a little.

**Paresh Naik** and **Sanjiv Shah**, for instance – both filmmakers based in Ahmedabad – agree that Ketan Mehta's 'Bhavni Bhavai' was perhaps the last memorable Gujarati film to be made in recent decades.

Paresh Naik who is currently working on a Gujarati feature film, 'Dhaad', had once worked on 'Holi' with Ketan Mehta, whom he describes as their 'guru', while people like Shyam Benegal were the idols of their generation of filmmakers. "We did a lot of work for the co-operative movement (in Anand) too and that became a part of our work and our ideology."

Naik says that while *Bhavai* is almost finished – Chimanbhai Naik is one of the last few veterans of the form – Gujarati theatre in Mumbai has a sizable presence. "Many of the plays that are hits in Mumbai travel to Ahmedabad and Baroda too. Sometimes, you see two teams perform the same play in different locations. There are some interesting one-act plays coming up, thanks to a college-level theatre contest hosted by Gujarat Samachar. It is fairly popular."

However, he says that now, the local film industry has gone to the dogs. "It is not just the Bollywood influence. Many of the financiers and even the artists have moved to Mumbai. Look at the sitcoms – many of the actors and producers are Gujarati. With Paresh Rawal, you saw a strong Gujarati accent being introduced on screen."

Sanjiv Shah, who made a Gujarati feature film 'Hun, Hunshi, Hunshilal', agrees that there is little happening in the Gujarati film industry. "For one, there just aren't enough films being made; not enough to nurture a loyal audience. The other factor is that Gujarati is very close to Hindi. Most people understand and speak Hindi and so they end up consuming Hindi – film and literature too."

If you'd like to test the filmo-mania metre in Gujarat, check out the back of auto-rickshaws in Surat.

Most vehicles have a rhomboid sort of space in transparent plastic, at the back; here they paste pictures of Bollywood stars. These are usually male film actors, doing their best to look intense or grinning widely. Salman Khan, Shahid Kapur, John Abraham and Sanjay Dutt are particularly popular at the moment.

Top
*A farsaan (ready to eat snacks) shop, model for the television serial 'Kudkudiya House No. 43'*
Left
*Naseeruddin Shah and Smita Patil in stills from Ketan Mehta's first feature film, 'Bhavni Bhavai', made in 1980*

# Making Space
## for the Mind

**Between** Ahmedabad and Vadodara, two of the largest cities in the state, there is a clutch of educational facilities that rank amongst the best in the country.

The **Indian Institute of Management** in Ahmedabad (IIM-A, as it is better known) is widely acknowledged as the best institute for management studies in India, and certainly one of the best in Asia. It is undoubtedly the hardest to get into, and more than 190,000 people apply each year for the MBA entrance exams. The institute was set up in 1961 by the Government of India in collaboration with the state and the support of industrialists. Vikram Sarabhai, the noted scientist, was deeply involved with the project and is held largely responsible for its creation and high standards. The IIM-A library, named after him, is known to be one of the largest management libraries in the world.

The **Mudra Institute of Communications**, Ahmedabad (MICA) is one of the best-known media institutions in India, and it specialises in developing communications management skills. Located on the outskirts of Ahmedabad, it focuses more on the development and management of communication rather than the basic vocational training, to serve the needs of the communications industry.

Ahmedabad is made more vibrant for having the **National Institute of Design**, one of the most prestigious design institutes and one of the

Title inset
*Eager to learn, the curious Gujarati spirit has resulted in the presence of some of the best educational institutions in the country*

Top
*The new Gujarat; A Rave party at CEPT, the Centre for Environmental Planning and Technology*

Left - Top
*The prestigious logo of IIM Ahmedabad adorns the arched brick wall at the entrance to this famous institution*

Left - Bottom
*NID, Ahmedabad - ivy league institution that has produced more artistic creativity than can be accounted for*

few that offers such a wide array of courses, genres and techniques on a single campus. It trains students in tie-n-dye and ceramics with the same dynamic approach as it lends to students of graphic design in new media. The city is also home to one of the National Institute of Fashion Technology (NIFT) campuses.

One of the oldest and most respected institutions is the **Gujarat Vidyapeeth**, a university in Ahmedabad founded in 1920 by Mahatma Gandhi, who originally called it 'Rashtriya Vidyapeeth' (National University). It was set up mainly as an alternative to British-run institutions, an extension of the Swadeshi principle. Since Independence, the university has modernised the syllabi but it remains committed to Gandhian ideals.

There is also the **Dr Babasaheb Ambedkar Open University**, which allows students a flexible route to higher education through distance learning. It offers thirty-eight programmes and caters to at least one lakh students. The university is headquartered at Ahmedabad but has a regional centre in Rajkot and plans are underway to set up another in Patan.

The **Nirma University of Science and Technology** is a deemed university in Ahmedabad, run by the Nirma Education and Research Foundation. It encompasses one engineering school, an Institute of Technology, a business school, an Institute of Management, one Institute of Diploma Studies, an Institute of Pharmacy, an Institute of Science and an Institute of Law. This one is a relatively new university and many of the colleges are yet fledglings, but the university has been growing steadily and continues to add courses.

Many of the educational institutes are a visual delight as well, for the central government had the foresight then to invest not just money and land, but also imbue these institutions with creativity and aesthetics.

For instance, a special marker about IIM-A is that the campus is full of baked-brick buildings, designed by architect Louis Kahn, especially invited and flown in from Philadelphia to create the campus. The newer constructions are more about concrete than brick, however. The new and old campuses are connected through a pedestrian tunnel that doubles up as a charming photo gallery.

The NID campus is similarly designed: low, wide, bright and sober at the same time, with its expanses of red brick, and visible signs of the creative spirit on display all around.

Another beautiful campus is the **Entrepreneurship Development Institute of India** (EDI) that was set up in 1983 and won the Aga Khan Award for Best Architecture in the year 1992. An autonomous, not-for-profit institute sprawling over twenty-three acres, it was sponsored by India's most significant financial institutions such as the IDBI, ICICI, IFCI and the State Bank of India.

The EDI specialises in helping set up other entrepreneurship development centres and taking further the commitment to research issues relevant to small and medium enterprises. In fact, it is helping set up similar entrepreneurship development centres in other nations like Cambodia, Myanmar and Vietnam.

*I studied at NID. Most design schools now focus on niches, such as graphics, because there is money in it. But at NID, the scale is much larger. There's textiles, graphics, but there's also ceramics. The facilities and faculty are still amongst the best and the students and teachers are not just Gujaratis. The National Institute of Design, the School of Architecture and MS University (the fine arts department) are the main artistic hubs in the state. What makes them different is that these institutions are the product of a certain entrepreneurial spirit along with vision. The MS University was made possible thanks to the Maharaja's vision, and NID and IIM had Sarabhai's vision guiding them. Nehru himself took an interest in setting these places up. The idea was not to give someone a job but to fulfill the nation's need for good architects, designers or managers.*

**Parthiv Shah,** graphic artist, filmmaker, photographer.

# Setting Up, Building On

The **Sarabhai family** is probably the foremost Gujarati family to be associated with knowledge – both in the sciences and the liberal arts – in independent India.

**Vikram Sarabhai** is already well-known as being the father of the Indian space program since he had helped set up the Indian Space Research Organisation. But he didn't stop at space or rockets or atomic energy or satellites.

He envisioned and helped set up the celebrated IIM (Indian Institute of Management) in Ahmedabad and also **ORG** (Operations Research Group), the first market research organisation in the country.

Fabric, design, dance and theatre – there was nothing he wasn't interested in. The Sarabhais are associated with the **Calico Museum**, a textile research institute, the National Institute for Design, and of course, Darpana.

**Mrinalini** and **Mallika Sarabhai** have run the **Darpana Academy of Performing Arts** very successfully over the decades, and together have been responsible for promoting classical dance at home and abroad.

Mallika Sarabhai, who is already at the indisputable zenith in her field, has done the nation proud by winning the Palme D'Or, the highest civilian award in France. And she is quite content to have no identity barring her nationality and her womanhood.

While talking about her mother's work, Mallika mentions the use of folk traditions in her choreography. In fact, sometimes, she uses only folk. "This is because she often wants to make some pieces accessible to people, especially if they deal with 'people' issues. Her dance-poem *'Is it a dream?'* is about a host of issues that face everyday people and she has avoided the use of classical dance completely. She also uses folk to show the still-enduring robustness of our culture in spite of the onslaught of Bollywood. "Folk hasn't really become a performance style, but with the increase in urbanisation, the rootedness of it is being lost."

She knows that the state is rich in folk traditions and, besides the *garba* and *raas*, there are several ritual dances of the Adivasis.

> "Festival dances like the *hudo, garbi*, wedding dances from north Gujarat, the dancing of the Siddis from Junagadh, the special dances of the Merh and other communities."

Nevertheless, she is disappointed with Ahmedabadi audiences, for they seem to be more tuned to classical music than any serious form of dance, classical or experimental. And what's worse, the audience doesn't pay! "They are still insecure enough to want to be seen at venues, especially performances, however bad or vulgar, which come from Bombay. And they are very *kunjoos*. Anything free gets a full house but they won't even spend fifty rupees for art (unless it is an investment!)."

As for the academy and vision, she simply directs you to her mother.

Title inset
*Students gather in the arched corridors at IIM-A*
Top
*Entrance to the Calico Museum, Ahmedabad*
Left
*Exterior of the Vikram Sarabhai Library, IIM, Ahmedabad*

Her mother believes that the vision Darpana started out with has already been fulfilled. She had wanted to promote classical dance, drama and puppetry in Gujarat, and she has done precisely that! Now, she intends taking it to the next level – which is to use these forms to tackle pressing issues such as untouchability and female foeticide.

Mrinalini married scientist Vikram Sarabhai in 1942 and founded Darpana in 1948.

When she started out, dancing as a formal performing art was virtually unknown in the state, especially south-Indian dance forms like *Bharatnatyam*, *Kathakali* or *Kuchipudi*. In fact, dance itself was frowned upon.

Through Darpana, she has helped change all of this. For the present, she sounds rather thrilled about the introduction of a form of performing martial arts – *Kalaripayattu* – in the academy, which the students are thoroughly enjoying.

There is a separate department dedicated to folk dances, including the Bhavai which is a part of the regular curriculum, and which is constantly drawn upon, to tease out new thoughts and ideas.

There are other women who are trying to use art for change, including poets. Rajendra Shukla certainly did not have Saroop Dhruv in mind when he said that Gujarati poets, since the Gandhi *yug*, have not used words as a tool of change.

**Saroop Dhruv** wields the pen like a weapon of the mind. She was associated with the well-known names in modern Gujarati poetry – known as the Hotel Poets Group and led by Chinu Modi – but she soon moved on to other fields that made larger claims on her voice.

She began to work with the underprivileged, the oppressed and the besieged. With dalits, tribals, minorities and women. She helped found the Samvedan Sanskritic Manch, a cultural group, and a media organisation called Darshan. In recent years, she has been helping nurture women writers through a network called Kalam. The role she sees herself play, as a writer, is best expressed in her own words.

"I: a poet
I cannot exist as a mere reporter.
Nor as a court bard.
I want to grit my teeth and speak without mincing my words
about this conspiracy
But for that
I must retrieve my pen
from a deep dark well –
my father's well,
my ancestral well,
the well that is the final refuge of women
who dive to their own shameful death.
I have to throw in a fishing hook, and pull out
my pen, a brand new pen
with my hands alone."

(Extracted from *Salagti Havao*, 1995)

*Art is all encompassing and it obliterates all divisions. It removes our self-made, self-imposed barriers of caste, class, language and community. It is like a fragrance that travels equally through a gurudwara, a church, a temple and a mosque. It is this space in which the breeze of freedom, of equality and of universality can easily flow.*

**Aditi Mangaldas**
dancer, choreographer.

Top
*One of the most respected gurus of Kathak, Kumudini Lakia*
Left - Top
*Dance Diva, Mallika Sarabhai*
Left - Bottom
*Fusing modern with classical to create an extraordinary space in dance; Aditi Mangaldas*

Men are not
blessed with
the kind of
common sense
we have. For
we understand
the language of
sorrow

better
(than men).

Kasturba Gandhi (who died in
jail in 22nd Feb, 1944, before
she could witness the birth
of an independent India)

# What She Said

**She likes sitting** on terraces in the old city, watching the Jagannath Rath Yatra go by in the tortuous streets below. She likes flying kites. She likes Sonia Gandhi and Aung Suu Kyi. But what she likes most of all is a challenge.

**Shivangi Chavada** of Ahmedabad, currently resident in Delhi, former classical dancer, now disaster management professional, says that she loved the challenge of building three hundred houses in six months, in Kutch.

Before that, she faced the challenge of working in a male-dominated sector. She was one of the first woman floor managers in an automobile showroom in Gujarat, a job few women take on even now. She was selling Cielo cars, with a degree in modern finance and industry tucked into her belt. She even managed a petrol pump for a while.

But, Shivangi had always wanted to be involved with the larger community, so she began to talk to drivers, mechanics, power-plant operators. And, like it was for many Gujaratis, the earthquake changed the course of her life. As she sat there, stunned, lost, and naturally, shaken, she got up to volunteer. She had already worked for Mr Sheetal Lakhia; now she began to work with his architect son. That was the beginning of the shift to disaster management.

"I found that this is what I wanted to do. Our villages are so vulnerable and yet so rich with traditional knowledge. Community knowledge is huge and using it is the only way we can have sustainable development. That's what I learnt as we rebuilt houses in Kutch. Modern culture is all about pace – how quickly you can do things. But there is more to progress and development than that."

> "I also learnt that our people are very resilient. We move on. Even if the government doesn't do anything, we will rebuild our lives. Even in the smaller rural pockets, there is a lot of self-esteem."

There's only one thing she regrets about having left Ahmedabad for Delhi. "What I do regret is that, in moving out of Gujarat, I am slowly losing my social networks. In Gujarat, everything is about networking: who you know, through whom you go. I must try and reclaim that."

Oh, one other thing she misses: *undhiyu*, *khichdo* and other festival food.

*"I don't ask for a charitable view of women or gender... but all said and done, ours is a male-dominated society. Few women come out, flying high and free. Most of them hardly leave their homes and cities. Our women are very adaptable and have a strong business sense. Yet, they end up working only in areas of comfort – like food, which can be done in the house. Their work is often not about money, but about pride. About being able to make money. But they are often trapped in home-based industries. SEVA does good work, for instance, but it is limiting.*

*"After the earthquake, I went on to study disaster management in Paris. Then, the Tsunami happened, and I went to work in the Andamans... At first, my family didn't get it. Why was I doing this - traveling and working alone in far-flung places? You see, I come from a fairly conservative family. My father plays the Israj and was a disciple of Pandit Jasraj. My mother is a retired professor. I was trained as a classical dancer and had begun to perform all over, at cultural festivals.... But I had realised, at some point, that I am only an average dancer. It was a tough decision, but I decided to go back to studying - modern finance. Also, I am also a bit of a rebel."*

Shivangi Chavada, disaster management professional.

Left
*Memories of Kasturba; Sabarmati Ashram, Ahmedabad*

# Celebrate Everything

**While Navratri** is most certainly the one of the biggest celebrations in the state, another important festival is the one devoted to Lord Jagannath.

The Jagannath festival is always associated with a *rath yatra* or a symbolic chariot journey. A chariot with idols of lord Jagannath (the lord of the world) is pulled through the streets by devotees and watched by thousands of others. The largest such *yatra* takes place in Puri, Orissa, but the one in Ahmedabad is the next-best in terms of the enthusiasm of the throngs, and the splendour of the chariots.

The word 'Navratri' literally means nine nights. These nine nights are devoted to the worship of Shakti – the Goddess of Power who is worshipped in all the various forms that female divinity assumes.

The ten-day festival, ending with *Dussera*, comes at a critical juncture in the farming cycles – just after the stultifying summer and just before the onset of winter. Navratri is also the time that devotees visit the fifty-two shakti-peeths, which are the sites of temples dedicated to 'Shakti' otherwise manifested as the Mother Goddess. There are three such sites in Gujarat: the Ambaji temple in Banaskantha, the Bahucharaji in Chunaval and the Kalika temple on Pavagarh hill in Panchmahal.

In Gujarat, the mother goddess (Ambaji) is worshipped through an energetic community participation in the *garba*, or the *dandiya-raas*. It is a form of folk dance, usually in a circle, and sometimes with a pair of short, decorative sticks. The whole state, indeed every place that has a few Gujaratis in the local population comes alive during these nine nights. The music and dancing goes on throughout the night in public grounds, residential colonies' community parks and even street corners. Over the decades, Navratri has become an increasingly high-profile event, with popular singers and musicians like Falguni Pathak being paid millions of rupees to perform at major venues and Bollywood film stars making guest appearances. Many of these nights are organised by professional event managers and dance competitions are par for the course. The best dancer, best dance partnership, best costumes and so on are regularly rewarded with prizes and they feature in the local newspapers. Women usually wear a skirt and backless bodice covered with mirrors, shells and bright embroidery, even caps, though in smaller towns and villages, sarees are more visible. In recent decades, there have been venues where each night has a different dress code. Men usually wear a churidaar with the traditional short, flared kurta, and caps or turbans.

Traditionally, the dancers would move in a circle around a *mandvi* or a *garbo*, which is a decorated pole or a metal structure lit with lamps, or a small image of Durga in the centre. You will also see a clay or metal pot with a coconut on top of it, since it is considered auspicious and the whole area may be decorated with palm leaves and flowers.

Navratri is also the setting for many clues to popular culture in the state. Fusion music and new fashions are immediately evident and almost every major change in the country's pop-cultural tastes is reflected in these nine days of revelry. This is also one of those rare occasions when men and women get to spend several hours together, under social sanction and romance blossoms often enough.

*Undhiyu comes in very different varieties. But let's classify them broadly as rural and urban. In urban areas, the papri is made with methi, green garlic, tomatoes, kopra and ajwain. It is all made together and served. In rural areas, these different elements are prepared separately and served to you; you have to mix it yourself as you eat, along with chutney. Traditionally, undhiyu was made in a clay pot, which would be sealed with flour and buried in the ground and a fire lit all around it. Now, you get readymade varieties.*

*As for festivals, like before navratri and Dussera, the faafda business in Ahmedabad crosses Rs 10 crore. People stand in lines for hours and hours, outside the most popular shops. Even I have to post my driver to stand in queue early in the morning. You can see people queueing up to buy faafda even at one o' clock in the night!*

*There are similar queues for undhiyu in the winter, and most specifically during Makar Sankranti. Several small corner shops will spring up just before the festival and they do roaring business.*

**Sheetal Lakhia**, die hard foodie

Top
*Large ferris wheels at fairs dot the landscape during festivals and celebrations, and many abound during the year*

Left - Top
*The joyous and upbeat garba on a night during Navratri*

Left - Bottom
*Joy is inherent in the Gujarati and it soars in celebration of life*

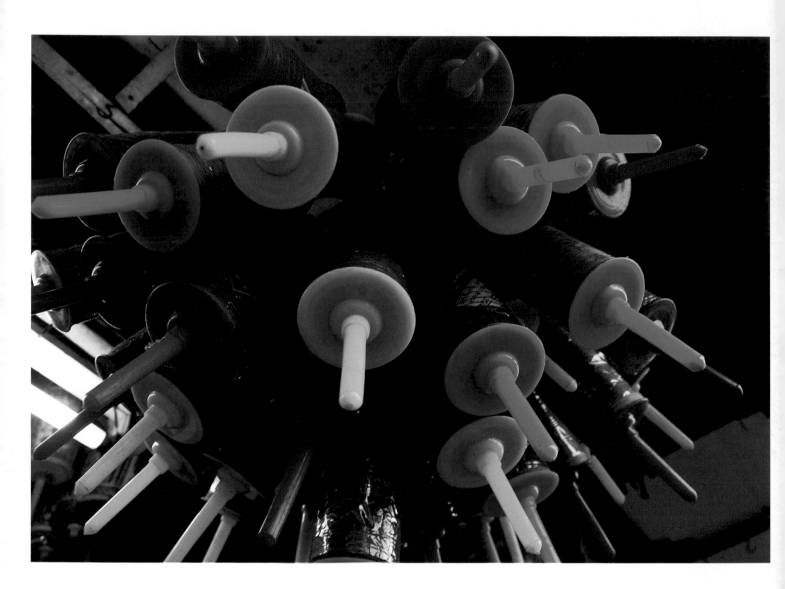

Top
*Gujarat rejoices with colour and it seeps into all celebration. Here a man makes ready the string for flying kites. During the festivals of Makar Sankranti kites fill the sky and you can compete about whose goes higher or whose is more beautiful, and of course, since all is fair in love and war, can you cut the other guy's flight?*

Left
*Spindles of the ready string, dyed and coated with fine glass powder*

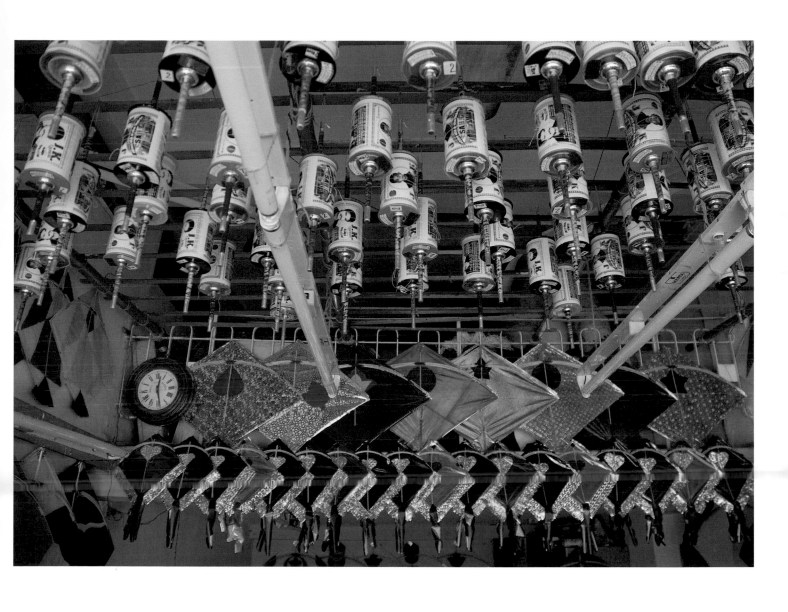

*Kites, kite-makers, kite-sellers, spindles, colour, gleaming, glittering shiny paper. The fun of kite-flying, the soaring up in the sky till the eye cannot see, appeals to the adventurous spirit of the Gujarati, children and adults alike*

# Where We Come From

**The word** "Lothal" , when translated literally, means "Mound of the Dead". It is unknown though whether this name bore any link to the fact that this site, upon excavation, would bring forth the secrets of the buried world and its dead.

Part of Ahmedabad district, the site was discovered in 1954 and was excavated by a team from the Archaelogical Survey of India over the next few years. Several such sites have been found in the subcontinent, many of which are now in Pakistan. On the Indian side, Lothal and Dholavira are the most prominent sites of a stretch that is called the Indus Valley Civilisation or the Harappan culture.

Archaeologists found something akin to a 'dock' that hinted at what would have been one of the world's oldest international trading route. Artefacts found here are known to have originated in West Asia and even Africa. The civilisation was highly developed with considerable advances in navigation, art, metallurgy and urban planning.

While many other sites of the Indus Valley Civilisation, such as Mohenjodaro and Harappa, began to decline, Lothal appears to have survived for a longer period. Not much is known about what eventually caused its collapse, but there are many theories – disease, floods, famines, war? Who knows?

Sometimes, it is good to press the pause button on life, on progress itself, and think of civilisation from the root up. Think of where we started and how far we have come.

Lothal is a good place to do this sort of thing.

Shells, beads, bone, ivory. Decor, skill, industry, organisation. Optimum use of minimal resources. Trade, national and international. Planned cities, ports, sewage, processing and distribution centres. Art!

Art. Tools. Jars, saw-blades, chisels, drills, mirrors, celts... Everything they needed, they had. Everything they wanted, they made. Whatever they found, they used. And whatever they used, they used with a skill and finesse that is breath-taking, even now. Perhaps, especially now.

It does take your breath away to think of people sailing in hand-made boats, with none of the modern conveniences of life-jackets, rescue teams, helicopters or digital navigation systems. To think of them sailing, not just once or twice, as an adventure, but on a regular basis, across oceans, to trade with what is probably now known as Oman.

That four thousand years ago, they could mine for metals, and import copper of 99.8% purity. That they could alloy it with 3-11% tin. That they made stone blades through what is now known as the 'crested ridge guiding technique'. Four thousand years ago, they could draw out a long core from the heart of a stone, with a series of weak points – remove the first blade and voila! You have many equal-sized blades, ready to

*Culture - is very hard to define. I grew up in Ahmedabad but have moved to Delhi now. I'm more of an internationalist in that sense. Yet, some things stay with you - colours, smells, sights... The food your mother feeds you as a child. That never goes away.*

**Parthiv Shah**, graphic artist, filmmaker, photographer

Title inset
*Main walls of the fort at Dholavira*

Top
*The ship-builders and their creations at Mandvi are descendants of the original dhow builders. These dhows plied the trade routes between Gujarat, Middle East, the East Coast of Africa - to Mozambique and Zanzibar*

Left
*Shards of pottery found at Dholavira*

be taken out. That they had an evolved system of measuring mass and length. Weights ranged from 27.584 grams (coinciding with the English ounce and Greek unilic) to 8.575 grams (equal to Iran's shekel), 100 grams and 50 milligrams, which is the smallest measure found anywhere in the world, during that time. Different people, different needs, weight systems. How easily they worked that out!

Looms. Thread. Bricks, spoons, chess-type games. Fancy shells spoons, distinct from ordinary stone spoons.

That they set up workshops for beads and metal-work. That, four thousand years ago, they probably placed as much of an emphasis on art and decoration as they did on tools and technology.

Poetry, story-telling, painting.

At Lothal, they buried their dead; sometimes in common graves. You cannot fail to be moved by the skeleton-couple that was found at the site in a grave. Who, how, how young? These things you will never know.

But a walk around the museum will teach you that perhaps, the more things change, the more they are the same.

Bullocks, fields, workers, bricks. Pestles, hammers, net-sinkers, fishhooks. Corn, wheat, peacocks. Still the same, as they were. Civilisation... sometimes you lose sight of what is just a rough beginning and what is at the apex.

Hirabhai, the cleaner at Lothal, will be very willing to play guide at the Lothal site. It is a very exposed site – both, to the elements, and to every visitor who may choose to stroll in. Hirabhai is right – it will take more than one man to protect it.

In the meantime, walking around the place, Hirabhai has developed a few theories of his own, about the Indus Valley Civilisation. He admits he is not educated, and has not been told any of this as fact, or even conjecture. But, in the absence of notices, plaques or trained architects on the spot, his fairy-tales must suffice.

"This, I think, would have been the women's bathroom. And these, for the men."

"Really? Only one for the women?"

"A large one."

"You think women had communal bathrooms?"

"I think so. See, this is covered. These ones, for the men, they are not covered. So only men would have bathed like that. Besides, women use more water. Three times as much as men do."

Suppress that giggle. He has more mind-maps to offer. A communal kitchen. A gutter. A bedroom. A hall. Water recycling units.

Something wistful creeps into his voice, as his feet trace an invisible sketch of a household. A dream home?

He shakes his gray head. "Once, men mattered; water mattered. Both were treated as precious."

Whether man - each individual - was ever held equally precious is debatable but water certainly was given its precious due, once upon a time. Not only were rivers held sacred, as they were across the whole subcontinent, but Gujarat also had several interesting water-conservation practices and money must have flowed out of the government coffers like, well, like water, since the rulers spent millions to build not just storage facilities but also to beautify and immortalise these conservation spots.

*Top*
*Bathing in the sacred Damodar Kund, Junagadh*
Left
*The guide tells you "that this is a large oven at the excavations in Lothal; you must be standing in ancient kitchens"*

देश
नाभसविवेध
परमारेश्वरः यःथग्या
सितिसम्पशातिसापतः प्रारा
विदंशाजनंश्विछुजक्षंप्ल
बाघायराज्याधिकारसंद
संज्जातिबुद्धसंज्जतथ्या
वतोंमानधबाविगायश्रद्धा
पराघाघहारिलिभ ४ विजयति
रिजराजाश्रीसद्भूमीपति
निसुक्तानिविनिर्मितानि
रुनोदिहिबालाक्षेत्ताधर्मभ
बनतिसुदंःसविकंक ताधें
नंद्वेजारःसंश्वरान
गाङ्गुदेहागब्रम्मा
लीलाविछुखवनवि
सखतनिवलजन
आनशालिलि
नपीश्वाल

The most ancient example of water conservation can be found in Junagadh. Sudershan was a man-made lake and successive kings ensured that it was repaired and kept in good condition, as is obvious from the rock inscriptions found nearby.

The inscriptions can be found near Mount Girnar, and you must stop and stare at what is older than anything you can imagine. At ancient languages and scripts, coded mysteries that took centuries to crack.

**Achyut Yagnik** and **Suchitra Sheth**, in their book, '*The Shaping of Modern Gujarat: Plurality, Hindutva and Beyond*' tell the story of a young boy from Junagadh who had managed to crack this code. All along, linguistic scholars had thought that the script was a variation of Greek. James Todd, a scholar, had sent samples to James Princep, who happened to be studying the *Brahmi* script in Orissa. Princep had figured out that the edict signified that this rock, and therefore Gujarat, was probably once a part of the ancient emperor Ashoka's vast empire.

Meanwhile, a young boy from Junagadh made copies of each letter of the script. **Bhagwanlal Indraji Bhatt** (1839-89) had learnt Sanskrit at home. By the time he was twenty, he had learnt to read some of the inscriptions on the rock. Yet, he had been able to prepare an outline of Gujarat's political history, tracing all dynasties in their proper chronological order, and an account of how various communities entered Gujarat. Sadly, Bhagwanlal was not well known to history because he did not know English; he wrote only in Gujarati.

The enormity of history can be overwhelming. It is funny how you can shiver a little at the sight of one large granite rock inscribed in *Pali*, telling the history of the Lake Sudershan, alongside emperor Ashoka's edicts in *Brahmi*.

An English translation speaks for king Devanampriya Priyadarsrim:

"But Devanampriya does not value either gifts or honours so (highly) as (this), (viz.) that the promotion of the essentials of all sects should take place.

But the promotion of the essentials (is possible) in many ways.

But its root is this, viz., guarding (one's) speech, that neither praising one's own sect nor blaming other sects should take place on improper occasions, or (that) it should be moderate in every case.

But other sects ought to be duly honoured - in every other case."

A wise, religious, modern man, King Devanampriya: one who is dear to the gods.

Lake Sudershan was not the only such water body that was maintained with such care; Kankariya Lake in Ahmedabad and the Khan Lake of Patan were other old man-made lakes. All of them had elaborate water-harvesting systems, with channels for transportation, filtering and outlets.

The Adalaj ki Vav is another such example of massive investment in water conservation. The marvelous five-level step-well, also called Ruda ni vav since it was built by Queen Ruda, the wife of Vikramsingh, was made in 1498, and the architecture incorporated traditional Hindu and Jain elements as well as Islamic designs. Full of exquisite carvings around the main entrance, on the columns and beams and around the small balconies at different levels, the place was clearly not meant to function just as a store. It was, and remains, a place fit for royalty.

Top 1
*Water channels at Kankariya Lake, Ahmedababd*

Top 2
*The carvings at Rani-ki-Vav, 18 km from Ahmedabad*

Left
*The Ashoka Edicts at Barton Library, Bhavnagar*

Page 164-165
*Breath-taking views of the Adlaj Vav (Rani-ki-Vav), awe-inspiring not only for their architectural detail and beauty, but their scientific innovative techniques and the foresight of planning the conservation and use of water*

Page 166-167
*The salt pans of Kutch reaching out into the horizon*

# Salt of The Earth

**The Rann of Kutch** has been described variously at different times: arid, inhospitable lowland, a wasteland, a flat, marshy desert full of desolation and salt, with nothing but the sort of scrub that animals won't eat; treacherous even.

'Rann' literally means desert and this part of the state is indeed part of the vast Thar Desert that stretches across the western wing of the subcontinent. In Kutch, this space extends tens of thousands of square kilometres from the Gulf of Kutch to the Indus River which is now in Pakistan.

It is the salt desert that gives India much of her salt and the local population have been working as professional salt-makers for centuries now. They usually work alone, and have to stand in salt-water for hours each day. It is famously known that when their dead are burnt on the funeral pyre, their feet do not get consumed by the flames.

One of the best seasons in the Rann is the monsoon, when the mudflats fill up with sea water and turn into an exquisite guest-house for flocks of migratory birds, larks and flamingos. It is also a breeding ground for shrimp and fish in the rainy season, when the salt-workers take out their tiny boats and go fishing for a living.

Kutch has been described somewhere as 'a schizophrenic ecological divide': there is the sea to the south and a salt desert to the North. It is a very fragile eco-system where drought seems to be an unwelcome guest that visits every couple of years with painful regularity. Unfortunately, the indigenous grasslands were destroyed when the government introduced a non-indigenous thorny bush in the region, hoping to stem soil erosion.

Traditionally, Kutch has been home to animal-rearing tribes, but the vanishing grasslands have led to extensive migration, with women shouldering the yoke of drought-driven livelihoods themselves. In recent years, some NGOs like **Sahjeevan** have stepped in, helping to make villages self-reliant in matters of water, food and fodder at least. They have sent trained personnel to study the soil and climate and to train the villagers themselves in watershed management and low-intensity irrigation practices. Women have been especially involved; in fact, their equal and absolute participation is a prerequisite for any village that wants to benefit from such training programs.

Water was not always a problem in Kutch. Since it has beeen a desert for centuries, it had made its peace with its climate long ago and the local people had devised a different conservation system, called *Virda*. This involved a shallow pit or a small depression in the ground. There was no attempt to tap groundwater because of the salty quality of the soil, which does not allow much seepage. Even if it did, the fresh rain-water did not mix thoroughly with the salty groundwater, and therefore, it remained fit for drinking.

The Kutchi rulers went a step ahead and even allowed for forest conservation. They had a tradition of reserving forest-lands much before the British. The British government in India had set up an 'Imperial' forest department in the nineteenth century in light of the need to manage valuable forest resources like timber and sandalwood.

*A lot of craft comes from the tribes. The tribes lived close to nature and their motifs and colours came from what they saw. In the desert, they took their colours from birds and animals – parrots, peacocks, flamingoes, horses. Bright pinks, greens, blues. A lot of black.*

**Asif Sheikh,** designer, textile revivalist.

Title inset
*Vivid Kutchi embroidery*

Top
*Strong splendid hardy women who live tough lives and wear the most exquisite embroidered garments and silver*

Left - Top
*Sunset at the salt pan at Kharaghorda, Little Rann of Kutch*

Left - Bottom
*Resplendent Harijan women in the Great Rann of Kutch*

They also set up the forest service and began to train officers in France and Germany at first, later in London, and eventually at Dehradun in India. Forests were 'reserved' to protect them, apparently, though it also served a dual purpose; rebellious tribes who lived in the forests and fought the administration were effectively barred from surviving in their natural habitats. Since Independence, reserved forests have been created to maintain the nation's green cover and protect the wildlife.

In the old times, the reserved portion of the forests in Kutch was called a '*Rakhal*' and nobody was permitted to exploit it commercially. Yet, the rulers were also sensitive to the needs of the poor and would allow shepherds or cowherds to graze there.

In the Rann, beware of what you do. You may leave no trace barring your footprints, but the desert will tell tales to those who listen.

Those who listen are called Puggee, Sodha (or Khojis, on the Rajasthani side of the desert). Desert detectives for centuries, these men can look at a set of footprints and can describe you, make informed guesses about what you're carrying and how well you're feeling.

The Puggees have helped the police in the past, by detecting intruders carrying RDX or arms and ammunition or narcotics. This community had settled on the Indian side of the border, after the 1971 war. They know their soil, they understand the human body and probably animal bodies too, and can even judge likely behavior patterns through your footprints.

From a 2007 news clipping in the Ahmedabad edition of the Times of India, here's an example:

"With miles of unending marshy desert land stretching before them, six Sodha community men sit on their haunches peering and poking at the ground...."

These six men are Savaji, Surtazi, Netaji, Padaji, Aliji, Swaroopsinghji and Vishramji of Zura camp. After a heated discussion, Surtazi Sodha Puggee tells a police officer:

"The intruder weighs 55 kgs, stands five feet nine inches tall, should be in his early thirties, has a small cut on his left leg. He is carrying eight kilos of load, he is tired, has run out of food and water and will reach Shakti Bet in the next three hours."

Where the little Rann begins, just beyond the mounds of salt and the bustle of trucks and labourers loading and scraping and filling, there is a curious medley of sound and silence. The wind whips and winds wound your body like a slow howl, like some live animal that cannot die and you aren't sure whether it is dangerous, for you see nothing but your own hair that has turned into a thousand fine whiplashes across your face.

Top
*Gandhidham; A salt factory where the salt is panned and brought in*
Left
*Rabari boys with their camel and on the salt pan at Kaladhungar*

But the silence – that is even louder than the sound. It rises from the very cracks on the ground. Even in the monsoons, the salt desert appears sullen, crawling with large, gaping cracks underfoot. It is a magnificent silence.

The one happy sight here is the *ghudkur* or the Asiatic Wild Ass. An endangered species, this animal looks like something of a cross between a donkey, a horse and a zebra. A dull brown shade, the ghudkurs almost melt into the hues of the Rann. But almost as soon as you arrive, they put in an appearance. As if on cue, they trot across your line of vision, but they do not come close and they do not let you, either.

If you step any closer than what they're comfortable with, they start walking off. You stop. They stop. They chew little clumps of dry grass or scrub, all the while keeping a very sharp eye on your movements. One more step, however slow or noiseless, and they start walking further away.

Peaceful creatures; a little like the Rann itself. Not visibly hospitable, but very sensitive. While they're not exactly shy with visitors, they aren't camera-happy and they certainly don't like any invasion of their personal space. You'd imagine that if they could, they'd wear a 'keep distance' sticker on their backsides.

Kanubhai and Shantiben's house is a well-known one. They are one of the few villagers in Vadagaon who keep horses.

Kanubhai has been trading in horses for the last fifteen years. His father had only one. That was when they lived in Mithaguda, on the edge of the Rann of Kutch. It was a very hard life and there was little food, so they decided to migrate here twenty-two years ago. They found a little land, some cows. And Kanubhai decided to indulge his interest in horses.

He tells you that there are at least thirty-six types of breeds and sub-breeds. You can tell a horse from his gait, the angle of his ears, the shape of the chest and the nose, and the hooves. Over cups of tea, he gives you a crash course on the habits of horses.

The most popular horse around here is the Kathiawadi; the last nawab of Junagadh was a great lover and collector of this restless, good-looking breed. Ears straight up, broad chest, big hooves. It is fast and when it wants to be (which is often enough) it is mean. It is a delight for those who like to handle danger and ride rough. For though it is beautiful, it panics easily and cannot be trusted in crowds. Yet, Kanubhai can sell a Kathiawadi for as much as Rs 5 lakh. On the other hand, there is the Marwari horse. A softer temperament, smaller build. It allows strangers to approach, unlike the Kathiawadi. It is the Marwari horses that are used for events involving some sort of public display, like a parade or for festive 'dancing'.

The Arabian horses are.... a dream, and Kanubhai doesn't allow himself such an expensive dream, but he does deal in Sindhi horses – smaller and more malleable – and other mixed breeds. His horse-trading has stood him in good stead. The elder daughter studies in a college in Gandhinagar. The future looks bright.

*In Kutch, the cuisine is very different. Because it was a dry, harsh terrain, which had almost no vegetables, the food included few vegetables except potatoes and tomatoes, until thirty years ago. Here, you have dishes such as tomato-sev shaak. In rural areas, the staple was thick bajre ki rotli and meat. (In Bhavnagar nearby, the staple is gaathiya and marchiya.) In fact, I remember, about forty years ago, in villages in Kutch, they used to put small pebbles in besan and fry them to eat as bhajia! Because there wasn't any other vegetable available at that time.*

Sheetal Lakhia, die-hard foodie.

Top
*Too fast to tame. Asiatic Wild Ass on a speedy retreat*

Left
*Tribals in Panchmahal tie messages on terracotta horses and fling them off trees. Messages on terracotta horses riding into the heavens everywhere*

# Honour, Pride.
## Steps and Strides

**Men of honour.** Men of few words. Men who worship the Mahuda tree.... the **Rathawas**. For them, bows and arrows are children's playthings. But men of honour, who favour the truth.

**Utpala Desai** started dancing only after she was married and had her first baby. Now, after her own daughter is married, she is working on her doctorate. Having studied dance throughout Gujarat – from the ubiquitous *garbo* to the little-known beauty of the dancing in forests of the Dangs or amongst the Koli fisherwomen.

She says that Gujarat didn't have an indigenous classical tradition for dance or music. Most of the dancing was folk and usually festival or harvest-related, which is why most of the festivals are concentrated between October and February.

"The most common, pan-Gujarati dance is the *raas*, or *daandiya*, or *garbo* or *garbi*. The *raas* was supposed to have come with the Yadav clan, Lord Krishna's community."

> *"Awake O Awake! Jadava, Krsna, cowherd,*
> *who will to the pastures go without you?*
> *Three hundred and sixty cowherds gather*
> *Who will the cowherd leader be?*
> *Curds, sweetmeats, sweetened milk*
> *Who O Who will savour?*
> *Tusker my Hari, mastered Kalinaga*
> *Who will bear the burden of the earth?*
> *With herds grazing on the Yamuna banks*
> *Who will play the enchanting flute?*
> *Enlightened, praising your name says Narsaiya*
> *Who will anchor us from this suffering sea?"*

(Extracted from 'Celebration of Divinity', a collection of Bhakti poems by **Narsinh Mehta**, and translated by Darshana Trivedi and Rupalee Burke)

The myth goes thus: king Banasur's daughter, Usha happened to fall in love with Krishna's grandson, Anirudh. She had him kidnapped and brought him to her own palace – which would be somewhere in present-day Assam, to the north-east of India. They got married without bothering to seek permission and Usha's father Banasur got so angry that he dragged off Anirudh and put him in a dungeon. So, Lord Krishna himself had to go over and rescue the boy; he also brought back the princess Usha (also called Okha; there is a famous dance-drama and poem describing a variation of the myth, called *Okha-haran*). It is believed that it was this princess who brought the *garbo* dance with her.

The fine variations are something Utpalaben can tell you about.

"The interesting thing is that the *raas* has so many variations. Each district has its own distinctive kind of *raas*, and you can see cultural and social differences reflected through this dance. For instance, at the Surendranagar fair (for shepherds), men and women both dance together, although the *garbo* was done only by women, according to tradition. The men dance the *garbi*, which is a more masculine, more vigorous kind of dance. The *raas* was also traditionally performed by men."

> *The Rathawas are a proud tribe. A beautiful tribe that puts up a very vivid performance at their festivals. The men walk up, playing the flute, wearing only a loin-cloth, and with white circles painted all over their torso. There is a belt of bells strung around their waists, which adds to the music of their step.*
>
> **Utpala Desai**, dancer, scholar.

> *Garba is the new pop culture. You see it all over Gujarat now. Youngsters are introducing new sounds and new rhythms in the dance. For instance, there is a new Daandiya – one step and a half. It is somewhere between two steps.*
>
> **Paresh Naik**, filmmaker.

Title inset
*Colourful bangles in the bazaar*
Left
*Pithora paintings on tribal walls in Jambhoghorda. A dying form of art by the Bhil tribe, these paintings tell folk tales passed down through generations. The tribals start from one corner of the house and slowly cover the entire space. Once the story is told, they will whitewash the walls and start all over again with another story*

"In Kutch, the Jats do the *raas* with only one stick. There is not much speed here; all the movements are soft and graceful. Only the men perform the *raas* here. And they are exceptionally good looking men!"

"The Bhavnagar Koli community performs the *raas* with a different sort of grace. They jump a lot. The Mers of Porbandar, who were a warrior community, show their roots in their stance. Their movements are almost like mock-assaults. In Jamnagar, the agricultural community performs the *raas* with a lot of steps that involve their sitting down. The movements remind you of the sort of work they would be doing – maybe cutting grass. There is a whole different variation on the *garba* which is called *besni*. This comes from Nalsarovar, a lake in Surendranagar, where the Padar tribe lives. Their dancing has steps which resemble their sitting and rowing movements in a boat."

"There are other dances like the *hinch*, which is performed during weddings, and during the *godbharai* (an Indian ritual much like a baby shower). The *hudo* is a form from Surendranagar where both the sexes join in a very vigourous kind of dance. Here, you see that men and women will touch each other while dancing. They clap their hands against each others', which was not traditionally permitted in all parts."

"In Pimpra, the Koli women perform a special kind of dance. It comes from their daily routine – they have limestone roofs that must be pounded for several days by groups of women, to make the roofing even and firm and water-resistant. Often, they also sing of their men who have gone to the sea. So, you see the Koli women dancing and singing with sticks in their hands, imitating the movements of the roofing work, singing of fishermen-husbands who have been away too long."

*Each tribe, of course, has its own dance and music. For many of the tribes, Holi is the biggest festival. It is celebrated for five days or seven. Then, there is mahua, music and dancing. Non-stop!*

*The Dungri Bhils of Sabarkantha dance the 'dhin taak', while in the Dangs, there is a performance known as 'kukana'. The Thakriya men perform a sort of rain dance – they wear ghungroos and play upon a tin box. The Siddis have their 'dhamaal' during the Bawa Pir festival. Besides, all the tribes have own kind of theatre too. Their own music. All tribes have instruments that are made from materials available in the forests. For instance, the Dangi tribals have 'thali vaadan'. They take a thali, put some wax and attach a hollow reed to it. This functions like a swarpeti, which catches the sur. They sing or recite to this accompaniment. It is not very different from a classical concert.*

*Generally, in Saurashtra, the dancing has a very specific meter; it is carefully choreographed. This is not true of tribal dancing. Their steps are simple, but they are in perfect harmony. With each other and with the beat.*

**Utpala Desai**, dancer, scholar.

Left
*Rabari shepherd family in Zainabad*

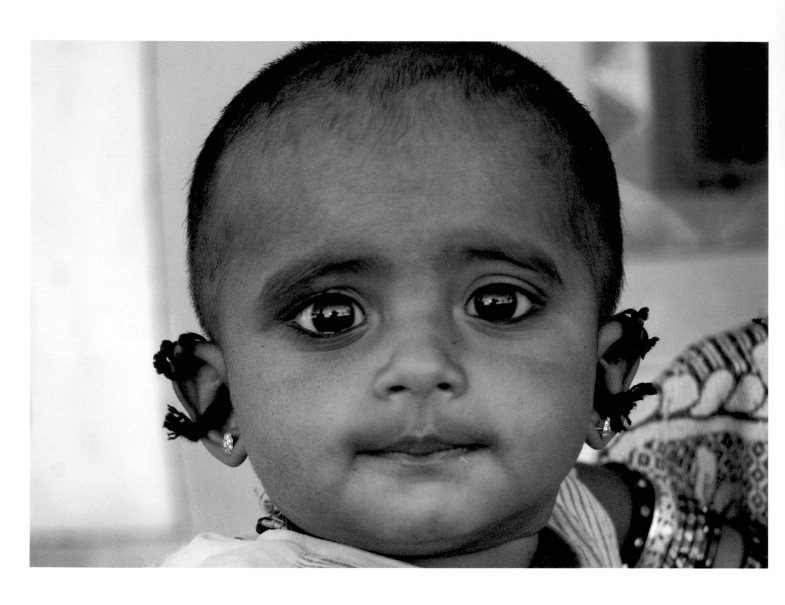

Top
*The mesmerising eyes of a little girl from one
of the last five families of the Jat tribe; their
origins in Afghanistan; brought up on camel's
milk, too strong for most stomachs, they are
nomads who move continuously, resilient to
the forces of nature and the arid environment*
Left
*At Hodka, the last outpost at the Great
Rann of Kutch; a tribal baby girl*

# The City that rose
## From the Dust

**According to legend, Rao Khengarji I** was the founder of Bhuj.

The warrior arrived at the edge of Hamirsar Lake, which a poor shepherd called Hamir had dug as a watering hole for his animals. The shepherd had demanded that while the Rao was free to build his capital, the lake would remain his own. Even today, the lake is central to the city.

What was special about Bhuj was that each profession had its own street, its own corner in the life of the city, and it stood near others who needed its services. In the book, '*Bhuj*', **Azhar Tyabji** writes that the old ways of building followed an unwritten code and a uniform aesthetic. Painting, music, dance and construction were very closely tied in Bhuj. There might have been an elaborate contractual system, which ensured both social harmony and economic interdependence. Even so, the arts were once a tool of urban development and not a superficial appendage.

He cites Prabodh Mankad, a gutter inspector in pre-independence India, who recalls his memories of the city and his understanding of how each street was named.

Divetia Street derived its name from 'divet' or wick, for it was the street of wick-makers who supplied the street lamps in the city. Needless to mention, this was the street that was lit up first, at dusk.

Volka Sheri is the street that follows the run-off route for storm-water. It was designed specifically to guard against floods. The design clearly worked, for the area around Hamirsar Lake never got flooded.

Jethi Mal Falia was the street of the jasti-mal or jethi-mal community. They were professional wrestlers and served as royal bodyguards. Talav Sheri came to be called Dr Mehta Street since Medhawala Gopalji Jetha Mehta lived there and wrote what may have been the first Gujarati novel: 'Karan Ghelo'.

Lungha Sheri was known for the Lungha community. These were Muslim musicians who performed each morning for Maharao Lakhpatji (a great ruler, incidentally. He built many fine buildings, including the Aina Mahal - the Palace of Mirrors. Under his rule, handicrafts and the performing arts flourished. He established the Brijbhasha Pathshala – a school for poetry and rhetoric – and Hunnar

Title inset
*Cactus flowers*
Top
*Aina Mahal, Bhuj; the Hall of Mirrors, and it seems of exotic glass lamps*
Left
*A modern Bhunga at a resort in Bhuj*

# Kala Shala, a folk arts school.)

## For three hundred years, the Lunghas played the *dhol-shehnai* at dawn, a performance called 'choghadia', followed up with a classical raga.

Machhi Pith was where fish and meat were sold. Bhatia Sheri was where the Bhatias lived, most of whom were traders, especially over sea routes, travelling to the Middle East and China. Kansara Bazaar was where Kansara or metal-workers lived, made utensils and sold them. Since wealth was measured in heads of cattle, you had a 'gau-dhan sheri' later known simply as 'dhan sheri'.

Maniar Falia housed the ivory-carvers, Maniyars. Salaat Falia was where the Salaat or builder community lived. The Hindu builders were called Salaat. The Muslims were called Manjothiyas and they lived off Majothiya Sheri. Together, they served as the architects of Bhuj. Kamaagar Falia was where the artists lived. Their name may have been derived from kamaan, since they specialised in the production of bows and arrows. That would also explain why they were settled next to the Vala Khawaas Falia and Rajput Falia, which is the soldiers' quarters, and Lohaar Chakla which is where the blacksmiths lived. The Kamaagars later took to painting and worked closely with the Salaats to decorate houses.

Dhatia Falia, Bhid Falia, Vania na Dela, Soniwad, Paburai Falia in Saraf Bazaar... Each worker with his own corner, a street of your own calling, near others you need or those who need you. Could there be a better plan?

As a traveler who travels right into the stories from history, you have to visit Lakhpat, the ancient port-city draped in a powerfully desolate and uninhabited stillness. This last town at the western end of India, at the border, is situated at the junction of the creek of Kori and the Rann of Kutch. The ruins of the ancient fort, with its rounded towers and gates, still surround Lakhpat, sentinels of a prosperous age when the town was a major centre of maritime trade, perched on the sea where the river emptied itself. The local story is that the place derived its name from the fact that trade generated a daily income of one lakh kori. Or, perhaps it was just named after its founder, Rao Lakha. But the Sindhu river changed its course, the creek dried up, trade dwindled and the lakhs stopped coming in. By the end of the nineteenth century the natives had moved away. The sea is still not too far but Lakhpat stands on a barren plain of limestone rock, and today, few families live in this almost deserted spot.

Monuments still tell interesting tales here. The tomb of Gosh Muhammad, a structure in black stone exquisitely carved with floral motifs and on the insides with verses from the Quran, stands testimony to the saint who was venerated by Hindus and Muslims alike. The Sikh Gurudwara at Lakhpat is a sacred place. Guru Nanak set off on his journey to Mecca for the Haj from Lakhpat, and the gurudwara was built to honour the event.

You don't just come away from Lakhpat. You emerge from a lost past into an alive present.

Top
*Portrait of the maharaja of Bhuj in Durbar Mahal with stag heads*
Left
*Portrait in Aina Mahal of the maharaja of Bhuj worked in real gold leaf and precious stones*

Top
*Gurudwara at Lakhpat. Guru Nanak,
the first Sikh guru made his journey to
Mecca from Lakhpat. He has said to have
left his belongings here 800 years ago*

Left
*Granthi (priest) of the Gurudwara with
Guru Nanak's 'Karao' (wooden sandals)*

# Wind, Water, Worship

**At Veraval jetty,** on Independence Day, where each little boat bears the Indian flag.

Outside Somnath, he stands, breathing melody. A dark adolescent boy, dressed in blue, looking out at the crashing waves.

He sells flutes.

The Somnath temple, near Veraval, is one of the most significant pilgrimage spots in the state. While the current structure was built only in the 1950s, the ancient temple whose ruins are present on the same site dates back to the 9th century, roughly. In fact, it is thought that a temple has always existed at this site, though not much is known about those constructions. There is a mention of Somnath in the Mahabharata and historical research suggests that the spot was a busy trading port and considered a point of pilgrimage even before the presence of a temple dedicated to Lord Shiva.

According to legend, the original temple was built by **Soma**, or the Moon God, as a measure of his gratitude towards his saviour, Shiva. The story goes that the Moon was so proud of his beauty that his father-in-law, **Daksha Prajapati** decided to punish him; he was cursed so that his beauty would wane. Another version of the myth is that Soma had twenty-seven wives, all of them sisters. He, however, had fallen so deeply in love with Rohini that he neglected all the rest and this angered their father so much that he cursed Soma. Lord Shiva came to his rescue but could not get rid of the curse entirely; he could only offset it half-way. Therefore, the moon waxes and wanes, waxes and wanes.

People believe that there have been seven temples at various points of history, some of which fell to neglect, some to attacks. As it stands now, Somnath is a popular destination with many millions of devotees thronging to it each year. There are several other temples in the vicinity, including a temple that marks the spot where Lord Krishna is supposed to have died, and a Gita Temple where the walls are inscribed with all eighteen chapters of the Bhagwad Gita, one of the holiest and most significant of religious texts.

Standing at the toes of an ocean, with the music of the roaring waves in the background, the area has quickly developed into a happy ground of family fun. Camels and ponies are harnessed to offer joyrides to visitors and stalls selling temple memorabilia, juice, coconut water and snacks cater to picnicking families.

Outside Somnath, she sells chikoos. Wears a kurta like a frock, gathered at the waist, and an unusual salwar – straight and loose, like a man's pyjama, but with delicate embroidery all around the hem. Ask her what sort of dress this is, and she says, "Ghachi. I am a Ghachi. Chikoos?"

"No. But I want a photo. May I?"

Outside Somnath, she sells cheap rings. Scrubbing silvery-metal-enamelled *bichhiyas* in soapy water. Squat beside her, ask her who she is.

"Bawaji. We are Bawajis. This is what we do."
"You make jewellery?"

*There are at least three or four thousand trolley boats. We catch pomfret, ribbon fish, some large fishes. The others are employed as carpenters and blacksmiths while many others sell ice – to pack and transport the fish. Each boat goes out with seven men, on an average. Each fisherman gets a salary of Rs 2000-3000 every month. The sailors are called 'khalasi'; there must be about 40,000 at this main jetty. The driver or navigator is called 'tandal'; he gets Rs 8,000-10,000. The owner's profit varies. He pays for the ice, diesel and food whch we carry with us. We stay in the water for ten days or twelve, and bring back five to six tonnes of maal. The slowest season is January-February. Our ladies also help - mostly to sort and cut and distribute.*

**Jagdishbhai Agya,** explaining the economics of modern fishing, at Veraval bandar.

Title inset
*Wind turbines, Mandvi Beach*
Left - Top 1
*The peaceful templed shore line of the bathing ghats at Dwarka*
Left - Top 2
*Somnath Temple, Veraval; they say you can draw a straight line from here to Antarctica without touching land*
Left - Bottom
*Sunday evening frolic at Mandvi Beach*

"No. We sell it."
"Who makes it?"
"Who knows? Somebody in some factory. We only buy it off the *seth*."
"How much for these?"
"Five each."
"Five?"
"You can have two for ten."

> *"Infinite glory of the Lord I praise*
> *How can these worldly men know?*
> *Protectors of religion, know not you,*
> *The difference between gem and stone.*
> *Mysterious to Vedas, Gopis access,*
> *Very few know the essence of this."*

(Extracted from 'Celebration of Divinity', a collection of Bhakti poems by **Narsinh Mehta**, the father of Gujarati poetry, and translated by Darshana Trivedi and Rupalee Burke)

Through the door you catch a glimpse of **Dwarkadhish**, the form of Krishna, bedecked in luxurious colour and glitter befitting a beloved God worshipped by thousands who come to the Jagatmandir at Dwarka to pray and receive blessings.

*Dwar* means door in Sanskrit, and besides being a gateway to the main land in the old days, Dwarka is considered one of the holiest doors to Hinduism, one of the four main spiritual centres in the country. Much of the song and dance, art and poetry of Gujarat revolves around Lord Krishna. There is a power in the expression of divinity which is almost palpable in Dwarka , the legendary home of Krishna and one of the most ancient and holy cities of India.

Explorations by the Archaeological Society of India reveal that the city has been in revered Hindu scriptures the Bhagavata Purana, the Skanda Purana and others.

Legend has it that Dwarka was submerged by the sea six times and today, you stand in the 7th Dwarka near the River Gomti.

Lord Sri Krishna, the much beloved incarnation of God Vishnu, moved abode in his later life from Mathura to Dwarka, where a well-planned city was built on reclaimed land – a city with wide roads, public forums and a good harbour.

Krishna's famous disciple, Arjuna, brought Krishna's family to his capital Hastinapur after Krishna's death, and in his words as reflected in the Mahabharata: "The sea, which had been beating against the shores, suddenly broke the boundary that was imposed on it by nature. The sea rushed into the city. It coursed through the streets of the beautiful city. The sea covered up everything in the city. I saw the beautiful buildings becoming submerged one by one. In a matter of a few moments it was all over. The sea had now become as placid as a lake. There was no trace of the city. Dwarka was just a name; just a memory."

The city is believed to have been re-built by **Vishwakarma**, the celestial architect.

The city is a devotee's delight with the many temples and shrines.

One of the most famous amongst these is the Jagatmandir temple, built of sand and limestone, which houses the Dwarkadhish – a form of Krishna. The temple originates from 400 BC and has been constructed and renovated many times since, through a long and colourful history, till today. You will be welcomed as you enter through the *Swarga Dwar* (the door of heaven), by a flag hoisted high on the temple tower which

Left
*Pilgrims from Okha enroute to Bet Dwarka, Krishna's lost city on the sea. You can barely see it at low tide and it seems submerged, almost like Atlantis, during high tide*

was built by Sambha, the grandson of Lord Krishna. And once you are overwhelmed by the *darshan* (sighting) of Dwarkadhish, the complexity of the temple architecture, and the view of the *sangam* – the confluence of the River Gomti with the sea, you will walk out of the *Moksha Dwar* (the door of liberation), quite awed with the experience.

The first philosopher and sage who taught the Advaita Vedanta philosophy in its consolidated form, Adi Sankaracharya, established a *math* at Dwarka. Dwarka Pitha, as the math is called is one of the four cardinal monastic establishments set up by him to guide the Hindu religion.

In Dwarka, there are also shrines for Vasudeva, Devaki, Balarama and Revathy, Subhadra, Rukmini Devi, Jambavathi Devi and Sathyabhama Devi.

To visualise how Lord Krishna lived, a boat takes you to the Bet Dwarka temple, built like the palace where the Lord lived. An idol like the Dwarkadish is also to be found here.

Also near Dwarka is Nageshwar Jyotirling, one of the 12 holy shrines of Lord Shiva.

To be in Dwarka on Janamashtmi is a special treat and a pilgrimage of its own. This is the birthday of Lord Krishna and is celebrated with great fervour and devotion across most of India, and especially in Dwarka and Mathura.

The day follows a routine based on Lord Krishna's daily activities - the offering of milk, a holy bath, adorning the Lord with gold, precious ornaments and rich garments, offering to Dwarkadish of specially prepared meals by the priests, and finally laying him to bed. Throughout the day there are series of prayers (*artis*) and devotees get a *darshan* of the Lord on special occasions during the day.

Hundreds of devotees from across India and abroad gather to welcome the birth of the Lord at midnight with much revelling, dance and song and cries of *Nand Gher Anand Bhayo- Jay Kanhaiya Lal Ki.* Most of them have fasted during the day and now break the fast with sweets and milk products.

Left
*The Dwarkadish temple at Dwarka, one of the holiest Hindu places of pilgrimage, and certainly the most joyous during the celebration of Janamashtmi, Lord Krishna's birthday*
Page 192-193
*A proud and patriotic fisherman in Okha*
Page 194-195
*Demoiselle Cranes in the Rann of Kutch*

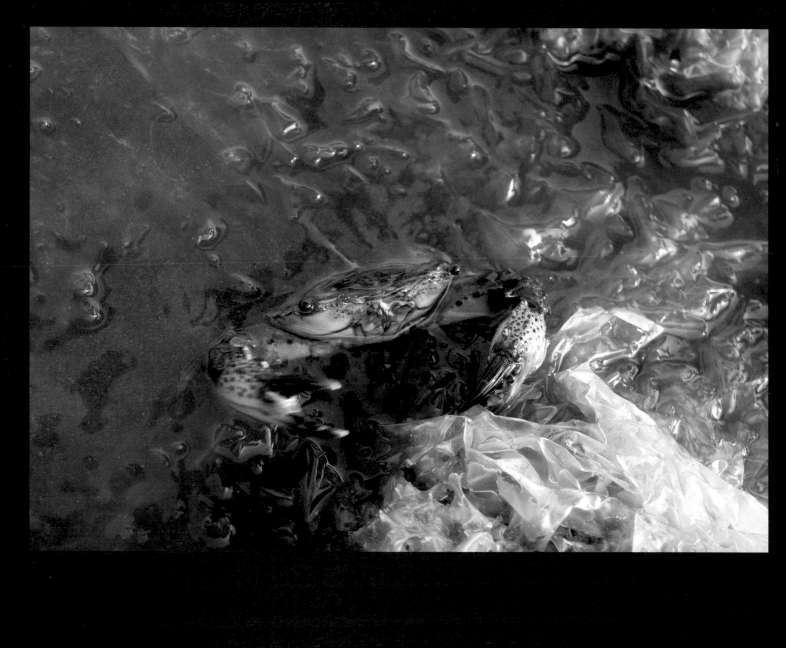

# Revenge and Riches

**The Jewel of Kathiawad**, Jamnagar is named after its founder **Jam Rawal**. Originally from Kutch, he appeared on the northern coast of Kathiawar in the sixteenth century. His father, **Jam Lakhaji** had controlled a small area called Terabanu in Kutch.

There is a well-known legend associated with the father and son and their fortunes, passed on by the bards of the kingdom. Jam Lakhaji was a brave warrior who was killed by two treacherous cousins, Tamachi Deda and Hamirji Jadeja. The two had envied him, especially after his successful handling of the siege of Pawagarh, which led to the emperor gifting him twelve villages. After he was killed, his son Jam Rawal escaped and swore revenge. Indeed, he did kill his uncle Hamirji, whose sons – Khengarji and Sahibji – escaped to Delhi and sought refuge with the Mughal emperor Humayun. They managed to gain Humayun's favour by killing a lion, during a hunt, just as it sprang towards the emperor. As a reward, they were granted a strong army with which they could fight to regain their kingdom.

Jam Rawal heard that the two princes were returning to Kutch with an imperial army. While he waited for the ensuing battle, the Goddess Ashapura appeared in his dream one night and told him that he would be punished for he had broken an oath undertaken in her name. She ordered him to leave Kutch. And, so he did.

Jam Rawal took along his best soldiers and traders and marched off. En route, he also killed King Tamachi, his other uncle, conquered the area and went on to establish Jamnagar as a new kingdom.

The modern city was built by **maharaja Ranjitsinhji** in the 1920s, and is the home of Ranjit Sinh and Duleep Sinh, the renowned cricketers, who lend their names to the coveted Ranji Trophy and Duleep Trophy. The city is a charming mix of wide streets and squares and ancient monuments with imposing facades. Famous for its silken and gold embroidery, bandhini and its silverware, in recent times, Jamnagar has been known for being home to the Reliance Industries refinery at Moti Khavdi village and the Essar Oil refinery. It is also well known for its **Marine National Park**, located nearby on **Pirotan**, a coral reef island.

"Hawker:
I may be called pheriyo but I don't roam;
Neither does my fate.
Even this wall sometimes envies me.
Not that I am scared to move.
If I had to move, Sonapur's not far,
A stone's throw. But I don't die.
Seven years I've leaned against this wall here;
Not missed a single day.
This wall, only this wall
I love; the only thing I love. Yet
Today it seems somehow
Like a wall seen maybe in dreams.
Till yesterday it envied me
Today it turns its face to go away.
Each year it gets a fresh, new whitewashed face;
Each year I look more crumpled and bedraggled.
Arre, were I a tree leaning over this wall!
Seven springs went by, but not a single flower."

(Extracted from 'Patro', in 'Coral Island', a collection of poetry by Niranjan Bhagat, translated by Suguna Ramanathan and Rita Kothari)

Title inset
*Tidal pools at low tide, Marine National Park, Bet Dwarka*

Left
*The riches of the sea; crab at Marine National Park, Bet Dwarka*

Page 198-199
*A natural breathtaking wonder of a life not often in view; some glimpses from the Marine National park, Bet Dwarka*

Page 200-201
*The birdlife at Gir : Storks, Lapwing, Magpie Robin, Cormorant, Eagle, Parakeets and Partridge. There's more there - the Park is a bird-watcher's delight*

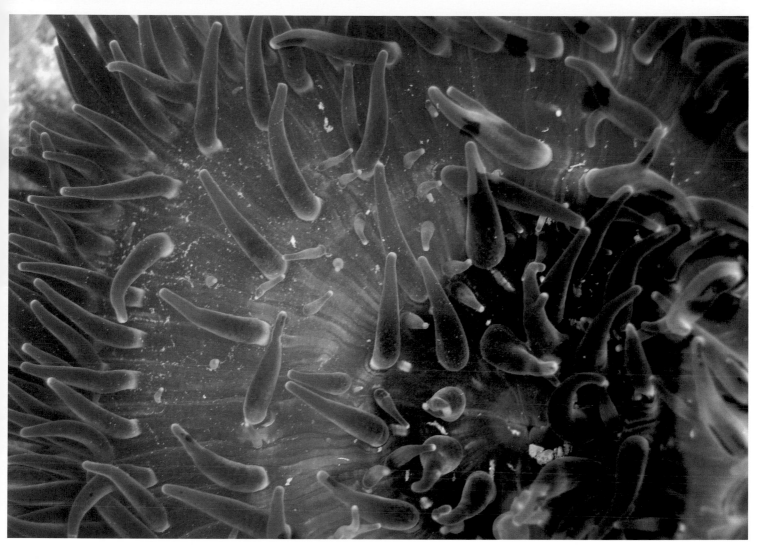

Top
*Colony of Lesser Flamingos at Nalsarovar*
Left
*Pair of Demoiselle Cranes in the Rann of Kutch*

# Old As The Hills

**Junagadh**:home to a mystic mountain; home to the earliest recorded history in the state; home to the Asiatic Lion in Gir; home to a tiny tribe that dances the *dhamaal*. Capital of the Junagadh State under the Muslim rulers of Babi Nawabs, Junagadh, in Gujarati, means 'ancient fort'. The city lies at the foot of Mount Girnar, abundant with temples and also a holy sanctuary of the Jains. On the way up to the peak of the mountain is a huge boulder on which emperor Ashoka inscribed his 14 edicts.

In Junagadh, the Durbar Hall leads to a silent, mournful scene - as if a royal court has just emptied the room, or as if the 'kacheri' has been left too long overdue. The plush silver is arranged all around a bright green-and-pink carpet that, a notice tells you, was woven by the inmates of the local jail. There are huge colourful chandeliers, imported from as far as Bohemia, Czechoslovakia, France... behind you, a container for scent warns you; it is made of poisonous coconut shells.

The walls are lined with larger-than-life portraits. Here, you come face to face with **Mahabat Khan III**, the last of the Babi nawabs of Junagadh, about whom you have read and heard so much. Here he sits, in all his resplendent glory, his many dogs at his feet. Some say he had a hundred, others say two thousand, though perhaps a more reasonable estimate is eight hundred. Others say that his love for dogs stemmed from the fact that a dog had once saved him from a cobra.

Pampered dogs, these were. They wore precious stones that were truly more necklace than collar. Pause here a minute, then, and wonder whether this was Roshanara, the privileged bitch who has gone down in history as the favourite one who was married off with great pomp and splendour to a fine dog, owned by the nawab of Mangrol. The *baraat* was greeted by two hundred and fifty dogs, decked out in silks and brocade. The groom was dressed, as befits grooms, and the bride was truly resplendent. Celebrations lasted three days, it is said. The wedding was conducted in complete earnestness, but the bride did not leave her 'parental' home with her new husband. In fact, after the marriage was consummated, Roshanara was not even expected to live with the dog. She retained privileges, as favourite bitch, which he could not hope to have.

The last nawab of Junagadh: collector of cars, patron of Kathiawadi horses, lover of dogs and protector of lions. Nawab Mahabat Khan III left India after the partition, leaving behind some wives, the lions in Gir and a lot of cars.

The last of his expensive cars – antiques now – can be seen around Junagadh sometimes. You see one lying in a ditch, rusting, just outside the city. You aren't surprised. The nawab had left Junagadh in a terrible hurry; there was no time to think of cars, or decide who ought to be given what. He left practically under siege for he had wanted his princely state to join Pakistan instead of India.

India responded by cutting off trade ties, triggering a food crisis and widespread protests. Jinnah, instead of accepting the request, had dilly-dallied and soon after, the nawab was left without a choice. People were protesting, led by politicians like Sardar Patel.

*The Maharaja of Junagadh owned 800 dogs, each with its own room, a telephone and a servant. A white-tiled hospital with a British vet attended to their ailments. When a dog died, Chopin's Funeral March was played and a state mourning was declared.*

*"To annoy the Raj whose airs and graces he resented", the Maharaja of Junagadh had his liveried staff dress his dogs in formal evening suits, mount them on rickshaws and drive them on British summer capital Shimla's fashionable Mall. "The women were infuriated, often feeling a dog's breath on their pale powdered faces as the rickshaws jostled for space on the way to Cecil Hotel for a dance. The Maharaja had a stormy meeting with the Viceroy and promised to keep his dogs locked away. He had to agree but waited until there was a ball at the Viceregal Lodge and ordered his servants to round up every crazed, lunatic pi dog in Simla. He set them loose in the grounds and was rewarded by the sound of horrified memsahibs shrieking like peacocks," writes Ann Morrow in her highly readable Highness.*

**Roshni Johar**, writing in The Tribune, 2003.

Title inset
*Trees at Gir*

Left - Top
*Maldhari tribesman; the Maldharis are a herders tribe who have lived inside the Gir forest for over 400 years, in complete harmony with their environment, even with the predators. It is now and so it has always been*

Left - Bottom
*Maldhari woman*

Eventually, he packed his bags, took his dogs, left behind several wives and settled in Pakistan. The cars rusting by the wayside remain: witness to his unceremonious, ill-fated exit.

## It was Mahabat Khan III who decided to rescue the Asiatic Lion from complete extinction. They had literally been hunted out of the world since 'trophy-hunts' were very popular with both the local royals and the British officers. The last nawab introduced about thirteen of them into the Gir forests, in 1907, and gave them his complete protection.

The lions in the National Park at Gir are particularly important since they are perhaps the last few specimens of the Asiatic Lion, sometimes also called the Indian lion. A few hundred years ago, they roamed wild all over the subcontinent, and beyond, up to and including the Mediterranean region.

The National Park stretches across over a thousand square kilometres of forest in Sasan-Gir and is one of the most significant protected areas in the world. Official estimates place the current lion population at more than three hundred, but most experts believe that the figures are lower and continue to fall, thanks to poaching, poisoning, accidental electrification and drowning, apart from the low fertility and genetic ill-health of the creatures which has been compromised by too much inter-breeding. Nevertheless, park officials have been doing their best to protect the lions and the park is closed to visitors in the late summer through the monsoon, which is their mating season. There are also plans afoot to move some of the lions to Kuno sanctuary in the neighbouring state of Madhya Pradesh, to prevent overcrowding in Gir.

**Uparkot**. The fortress up there. The mists lazily draping and undraping Mount Girnar, across your gaze.

The guide is a slip of a boy – a fifteen-year-old called Bhavin. The son is celebrating Independence Day by working in his father's domain. Quickly picking up hints, remembering the more outrageous stories, mentally marking the bits that most intrigue tourists, using his own boyish imagination in the absence of fact.

He leans in at the car window, rattling off a little ditty. "Nine kilometres long. One kilometre worth of walking. Thousands of years of history. Bolo?"

Before you can say 'no', he begins telling you – for a hundred rupees – that "the Junagadh fort, Uparkot, has known 33 kings whose names began with 'ra'. Like 'Rakhenga'."

He takes you to the entry point of an escape tunnel which a long-dead queen, whose name also began with 'ra' – Ranak Devi – had allegedly used to escape. "There was another king – Sidhraj Jaisingh. He attacked this fort because he had once been engaged to this queen but she went off and married Rakhenga. The siege lasted twelve years and Rakhenga

Left
*The famous Asiatic Lion ( in this case, Lioness), Gir National Park*

was betrayed by his own men, when they were sent out to get grain. He was killed by Sidhraj, who even smashed the heads of the two little princes – right here! On this black stone."

How does he know all this? Who told him?

"I just know. Listen, the queen escaped as the battle was lost. But at the other end of the tunnel, she thought, she could not escape. So she became a sati. There was a spark at her toe, it travelled all the way up to her head and she burst into flames."

Really?

"Yes, really. Now, come and see the Adi-Chadi Vav. Cut out of natural rock. There are 162 steps. The king got this well dug but he didn't find water, so the priest said, two young girls must be sacrificed. There were two sisters, Adi and Chadi who sacrificed themselves. They put knives in their stomach – like this!"

He makes a stabbing motion, not unlike the actor, Aamir Khan in 'Qayamat Se Qayamat Tak'.

And how does he know that they used a knife? He will not tell.

"Now, see this tree. If you go down to the vav, and take a mouthful of that water and don't swallow it; run upstairs again – 162 steps – and spit it at the roots of this tree, you are sure to get a big bungalow, air-conditioned and all. But not in this life. It is a way of securing your future in the next life. Make advance bookings, upar."

He points to the sky, grins at your grimace when you look at the colour of the water at the bottom.

At the Buddhist Caves, he is silent. He doesn't know much about Buddhist art or monastic practices, but makes up for what he doesn't know by cooking up little details. At one little cell, which is equipped with a modern barred metal door, clearly not part of the original structure, he declares, "And this is the lock-up! When people disturbed the monks' meditation, they would lock them up, in this room."

You cannot help laughing. He sulks and hides behind a pillar.

Sidharaj, greatest of the Solanki kings. The one who conquered all of Kutch, Saurashtra and even Malwa. Renowned for his justice and valour.

One incident stands out as a sign of the lengths he was willing to go to, to ensure that justice was done. The Turkish chronicler Mohammad Ufi has recorded an instance of when a mob attacked a mosque in Cambay, during the reign of Sidhraj Jaisingh. When the complaint reached him, the king set forth in disguise, to investigate the matter. He found truth in the complaint and ordered that the guilty be punished, and even had the mosque rebuilt at royal expense.

**Sidhraj Jaisingh**. There is no way of knowing, it seems, whether the story told by the over-imaginative guides at Uparkot is true or not. Historians say there is no evidence, yet the story remains popular. And why not? It has all the crucial ingredients of a Bollywood classic – a romantic tug-of-war combined with a real war! Besieged lovers, betrayal, despair, the ultimate sacrifice!

In fact, if legend is to be believed, Sidhraj, the great Solanki king, tried to acquire a reluctant woman not once but twice. And he failed, twice.

The story of **Jasma Odhan** is the better known legend. It is said that Jasma was a labourer woman of the Odh community, traditional tank-diggers, who was working at a site in Patan. Sidhraj set his eyes and his

heart upon her, but she rejected his advances. A king does not take easily to rejections, one assumes. In any case, it all ended with Jasma taking her own life. This story, in fact, has been embellished and has several variations across northern India. Ekjute, the theatre troupe, has already done a stage version in the traditional *bhavai* form.

It is a very romantic idea. To wake up with music, sleep with music, mark the passing of the day's hours with music... Just the sort of thing kings and queens would do. Just the sort of thing they did.

That's what the *Naubatkhana* is about: a house of time and music. The place takes its name from the Persian 'naubat', or the *shehnai*, but was also home to drums. At daybreak, the musicians would play the first wake-up notes, rise into a *raaga*. The last notes were played as the day ended and the capital's twelve gates were closed for the night. Come rain, come shine, the naubatkhana would not be bereft of music, for the silence of the musicians was a sign of defeat in battle.

It is not only in Junagadh that you find the naubatkhana. In Bhuj, this special room remained intact until the earthquake. In Ahmedabad, it remains so, just outside the east gate near the Jama Masjid. At a long-dead king's tomb, the Badshah no Hajiro, even today the Naubat musicians sometimes strike up a melancholy raga. For old times' sake. Or, as a passing nod to history.

Top and Left - Top
*6th Century Buddhist Caves*
Left - Bottom
*The Baoli (well) cut out of rock at the Junagadh fort complex*

# Accustomed to Valour

**Valour comes** to a people in many guises. Warriors and conquerors like Sidhraj Jaisingh or Mahmud Begada stand at one end of the spectrum of courage. Mahatma Gandhi is the other end.

Another face is the one belonging to the traditions of the Charans and the Bhats.

Theirs is a curious sort of valour for it threatens nobody, either financially or physically, except themselves; relying on an inherent human sense of honour, they perform *tragu*, a sort of sacrifice. Whether they stopped at simply cutting themselves or whether all *tragu* incidents led to suicide, it is hard to tell. But the community underwrote guarantees with their own blood.

For instance, if somebody borrowed money and refused to return it, the Charan who stood surety for the loanee would cut himself or threaten to set himself on fire. The community was known to stand surety for travellers too, to protect them from highwaymen. If attacked by dacoits, or even if robbers tried to take away the livestock, the village Charan would commit *tragu*.

From a position of moral strength and at the risk of his own life, he'd exert pressure on others to act with honour. Little wonder then that the Charans stood as surety for agreements between kings, feudal lords, landowners and even robbers.

Interestingly, 'tragu' is only performed when the concerned party is not really an enemy. If they think of somebody as the enemy, they are just as willing to pick up arms and rush into battle. Self-inflicted hurt or, depending on the nature of the injury, a suicide bid is reserved for those who have once been friends, people worthy of trust.

*Tragu* was banned by the British in the early years of the nineteenth century, and slowly, the tradition began to die out. But a visit to parts of Kutch will testify to the esteem in which the tradition was held, through a 'palia' or a memorial stone, often at the edge of the village. Many of them bear a crude picture of a man stabbing himself with a dagger

The women of the Charan community were also quite remarkable. They were just as willing to perform *tragu*, even if it was for a purpose no larger than the life of a rabbit. **Punai Mata**, according to Charan legend, had killed herself when she found herself unable to protect a rabbit that had taken refuge with her. A woman who sacrificed her life was supposed to be venerated as a mother-goddess.

The community's men are called *devi-putra*: born of the Goddess. They worship, in one form or the other, a mother-goddess. Sacchiya Mata, Karani Mata, Bahuchara Mata, Bhut Bhavani, Hinglaj Mata, Khodiyar Mata, Sonal Mata... the feminine in her myriad manifestations of truth, war, wrath, jealousy, non-violence, desire.

So, naturally, the women who give birth to brave men were not expected to be frail or fearful or squeamish. Animal sacrifice was a part of the festivities at the Mata temples, including Ambaji, and during Navratri, a bhainsa (male buffalo) was offered to the Mother Goddess. According to mythology, the goddess had warred for nine days and nine nights against Mahisasura, a demon who had taken the form of a buffalo. She

Title inset
*The Armoury, Laxmi Vilas Palace, Vadodara*
Left
*An armed and decorated bridegroom on his horse on the way to his wedding, Zainabad*

emerged victorious and the ritual sacrifice of the buffalo is thus part of the celebration. The first cup of blood from this sacrifice was usually offered to a Charan woman – the embodiment of *Shakti*.

The other thing the Charans were known for was their poetry. There is a whole distinct branch of literature known as Charani Sahitya. It included songs of praise for God, for a royal patron or the bounty of nature, descriptions of battle, songs of love, *marasiyo* (mourning songs for dead soldiers or companions). But they also sang songs that criticised their own powerful rulers, which are called *uplambho*, and biting satirical verses called *thekadi*.

One of the greatest Charan poets in recent times was **Dula Bhaya Kag**, who had his own facet of valour and honour. It is said of him that he refused to write poetry that he did not believe in.

આવકારો મીઠો આપજે

તારા આંગણિયા પૂછીને જે કોઈ આવે રે..
આવકારો મીઠો આપજે રે જી..
તારે કાને રે સંકટ કોઈ સંભળાવે રે..
બને તો થોડાં કાપજે રે જી..

માનવીની પાસે કોઈ, માનવી ન આવે રે..
તારા દિવસો દેખીને દુનિયા આવે તો..
આવકારો મીઠો આપજે રે જી..

કેમ તમે આવ્યા છો? એવું નવ પૂછજે રે..
એને ધીરિ રે ધીરિ તું બોલવા દેજે રે..
આવકારો મીઠો આપજે રે જી..

વાતું એની સાંભળીને, આડું નવ જોજે રે..
એને માથું રે હલાવી હોંકારો દેજે રે..
આવકારો મીઠો આપજે રે જી..

'કાગ' એને પાણી પાજે, ભેળો બેસી ખાજે રે..
એને ઝાંપા રે સુધી તું મેલવાને જાજે રે..
આવકારો મીઠો આપજે રે જી.

(Kavi Dula Bhaya Kag, better known as **Kag Bapu**)

There are stories about how Dula Kag was drawn into the bhoo-daan movement in the 1950s.

**Vinoba Bhave** had initiated this movement for taking land as a donation - 'daan' - from big landowners and redistributing it amongst the landless. The gentleman who was responsible for bhoo-daan in this region was a great fan of Kagbapu and he went to him, asking for a poem that would encourage the Gadhavi community to give up some of their land. The poet refused on the grounds that the Gadhavis are, by and large, marginal farmers and couldn't afford to donate their land. But over time, Kagbapu allowed himself to be persuaded. He wrote that poem as gift for the movement, but first, he gave up all his land. Because he would not write without honour.

Valour, as you see, has many faces.

# Telltale Curls

**Finding Bawa Gorni mazar** takes a lot of looking around and asking around. Nobody quite seems to know who the Baba was, who the Siddis are and where they live. Until finally, a white-capped auto-driver asks 'habshi?'

You find it, tucked away in a little corner at the end of a narrow street. This little community of Siddis is descended from the Africans who may have come here as traders, slaves or mercenaries. There is no way of knowing. The Siddi Syed mosque – more specifically, the *jaali* – is well-known throughout the state for the magnificent wonder it is.

The Siddi Syed (also spelt as Saiyyad) ni Jaali is an intricately carved screen which is locally referred to simply as 'The Jaali' and is recognised world-wide as the unofficial symbol of Ahmedabad. It is one of the best examples of Indo-Saracenic architecture and is part of the Siddi Syed mosque near Laal Darwaza. This mosque was once part of the fortified bastion built by Ahmed Shah in the fifteenth century and it was built by **Siddi Syed**, a brave and loyal general working under the first sultan of Ahmedabad. What makes this stone screen unique is the exquisitely delicate and intricate filigree work with motifs drawn from a combination of Indian and Islamic traditions. The twin screens show a central tree with complex, curved tendrils.

Little is known of the man who built it – in 1572 AD – an Abyssinian who served **Rumi Khan**, the son of the Governor of Surat, later a member of the personal retinue of Bilal Jhajhar Khan, also an Abyssinian general. Siddi Syed served in the army of the last sultan of Gujarat, acknowledged as a learned man who built a large library. He died in 1576 and was buried here.

You might find the portrait of another Siddi, **Ahmed Khan**, the nawab of Janjira, in the museum at Junagadh, but others from the community know little of who they are and from where they came and how long they've been settled here.

Their only sense of identity is their hair – tight curls that mark them out as *habshi*, or negro. Their only faith revolves around Bawa Gor, an old Pir about whom, again, they know little. But they celebrate a wonderful festival during the rainy season, on the 11th of Rajab (according to the lunar calendar). A *jalsa*, or celebration, that includes large drums and the *dhamaal* dance. There are about a hundred and fifty households in the state, and only about five families in this area of Junagadh.

**Hallu Ma** is the current caretaker of the tomb. Before her, it was her father and her husband who served. After her, her sons or daughter-in-law will. They have few rituals.

Rituals cost money, and there isn't any. Most of the women work as domestic maids in others' homes. Most of the men work as labourers or sell cheap things on carts at the local markets. Keeping the *mazar* going is about all they can do. The tombs of Maye Misra Ma, Bawa Gor's sister, and Ya Siddi Mukta Ghazi, his brother, are on their way to collapse.

Title inset
*The 'jaali' of the Tree of Life*

Left
*A lively Siddi boy. A large contingent of Siddis assimilated with the Maldharis at Gir and one village is still negroid in their features, clues to these visitors long long ago*

# A Willful Heart

**One interesting facet** of Gujarat is that barely fifteen percent of this geographical area was ever directly under the control of the British. There were at least two hundred small princedoms and a few large kingdoms, such as Baroda.

**Vadodara**, better known as 'Baroda', is the third biggest city, by the size of its population, after Ahmedabad and Surat.

Vadodara was founded on the banks of the River Vishvamitri, which is supposed to be named after the saint – the rishi – Vishvamitra, who finds mention in the ancient epic text, the Mahabharata. It is believed that the site was initially a small village near a town called Ankottak (now called Akota). And then the flooding waters of the Vishvamitri forced the villagers to cross to the eastern bank and take refuge near a cluster of Banyan trees. The village was called *Vadpatrak* (leaf of the Banyan), which later grew into *Vadpatra*, which grew into Vadodara. Some say that Vadodara is a corruption of the Sanskrit word '*Vatodar*' (the heart of the Banyan).

It is also said the city was once called Chandanvati, after the king Chandan, who came from the Dor tribe, or Viravati. In any case, the English merchants called the town 'Brodera' and later, Baroda. The name stuck until 1974, when the state government went back to the older version, Vadodara.

Before the Gaekwads conquered Baroda, it was ruled by the Babi Nawabs, who in turn had derived their power from the emperor in Delhi. When the Mughals declined, Pilaji Rao Gaekwad brought the Maratha forces to this part of Gujarat and captured power. At first, Pilaji just collected revenue on behalf of the Maratha Peshwa, but soon he carved out a kingdom for himself. The Gaekwads remained in power, at least nominally, until 1948.

However, in 1802, the new Gaekwad king sought help from the British, to save his throne and entered into a treaty with them. This ensured that while he remained 'maharaja', he had to recognise the British as a paramount and superior power and could hardly take any independent decisions. **Sayajirao Gaekwad III** was the only ruler to defy the British and also the only one who set about modernising and reforming his state with real compassion and a sense of justice.

It is also thanks to his investment in art and education that Baroda came to be known as Sanskari Nagari or the cultural capital of the state. We owe him the beautiful Lakshmi Vilas Palace and the Maharaja Sayajirao University (MSU), which is well-regarded for its fine arts and performing arts departments.

The Fine Arts Faculty at **MS University**, Baroda, has been a hub for dozens of talented artists over the last few decades and was one of the first to offer a fine arts degree. Renowned artists like **Ghulam Mohammad Sheikh** and **Bhupen Khakkar** have lived and worked here; teachers like **Nandlal Bose** and **NS Bendre** have spawned a whole generation of new artists, and significant names like **Shibu Natesan**, **Dhruva Mistry**, **Rekha Rodwittiya**, **Nilima Sheikh** and **Surenderan Nair** are associated with a collective influence that has been described as the 'Baroda School' of art.

*I did my doctoral research in Baroda. The Gaekwad had used modern buildings to modernise the state. He brought in a British architect and the famous urban planner Patrick Geddes. The Gaekwad was a very progressive ruler and used (town) planning in very interesting ways. He used public works in conformity with his progressive philosophy and through the architect, he had introduced newer services into the older parts of the city.*

Jagan Shah, Delhi-based architect

Title inset
*Rolling the pitch at Moti Bagh Cricket grounds, Vadodara*

Left
*The ostentatious Laxmi Vilas Palace at Vadodara; a confusion of architectural styles as you can see right here*

The Baroda School is known for a narrative-figurative style, which became popular in the 1970s and 80s. Through this phase, the artists began to tell stories, their own or that of others in the city and the larger country. This was a remarkable phase in which they broke away from the western-leaning style of painting taught at the JJ School of Art in Bombay, while also trying to revive indigenous forms of painting such as various tribal styles or the Mughal miniature style. The stories and figures slowly began to leave their canvases in the 1990s, and installation art, pop art, kitsch, minimalist styles took hold of the artists' imagination.

Artists like Bhupen Khakkar don't teach as part of the faculty but his influence and sheer presence demands notice and recognition as part of the artistic landscape of this school. He has been described as 'confrontational', 'irreverent' and 'a chronicler of the middle class and the world of ordinary human beings' who changed the visual vocabulary for many students in Vadodara.

One of the most significant aspects of the Baroda School is that they look upon art as a vocation. Nilima Sheikh has written, in 'Contemporary Art in Baroda' that while some teachers brought to Baroda the lineage of Tagore's Santiniketan, they also brought caution with respect to the "freezing of creativity, the degeneration of ideology into dogma and stereotype." She believes that the explosion of creativity was made possible with the infusion of the unworldly spirit of the Santiniketan artists within the down-to-earth Gujarati reality.

Even in the early days of the university, there was a definite emphasis on learning from various sources. Maharaja Sayajirao Gaekwad had invited Raja Raja Ravi Varma to Baroda and fourteen canvases by the legendary master are kept there still, a source of great pride for the citizens. Kalabhavan was established in the late nineteenth century as a training ground for traditional arts and crafts but there was a great deal of influence from all possible schools.

Experimentation, fearlessness and change were some of the lessons they must have absorbed from their teachers and mentors. Ghulam Mohammad Sheikh, for instance, whose earlier work so obviously leaned towards tradition, is now experimenting with multimedia and Photoshop, not just paper and canvas. **Chintan Upadhyay** is the quintessential rebel of the Baroda School, using not just paint but sculpture, installations, interactive art. Nilima Sheikh uses stories, poetry, elements of theatre. **Vivan Sundaram**'s art extends to painting, sculpture, printmaking, photography, installation and video.

Since students and teachers came from all over the country, they brought their own influences and traditions with them. This led to a great co-mingling that took the school beyond mere revivalism or imitation. Authority was never overbearing and students chose to express themselves through a close, critical eye.

**Manu Parekh** isn't really a product of the fine arts faculty, for he studied at the JJ School of Art, in Mumbai, but is one of the most successful artists from Gujarat living today. While he supported himself for years through Gujarati theatre in Ahmedabad, his influences have come from other Indian cities like Kolkata, Varanasi and Mumbai as well.

Gujarat owes much to Baroda: the best artists, deep research and scholarly work, and one of the best-known universities in the country.

Baroda owes it all to **Sayajirao Gaekwad III**, who assumed full monarchial powers in 1881, and set about transforming Gujarat with a determination and vision rarely seen in any time or region.

The kingdom of Baroda at that time described an area almost equal to what was called 'British Gujarat'. The Gaekwad resisted all attempts by the British to control his state and he refused to follow Lord Curzon's

*In Baroda, the bar is set high. Works and artists are expected to be extraordinary because the past generation has set very high standards.*

Art critic **Ina Puri**, in an interview to the Indian Express.

*Faces excite me... My stay in Calcutta and Benares and my travel through Indian villages have given me a portfolio of different human faces. There are elements of theatrical language when I do a face against a dark background. When I do a face it is also a landscape... the Indian face is poised between faith and fear.*

**Manu Parekh**, in an interview with art critic Ela Datta.

Top
*Statue of maharaja Sayajirao, with the MS University in the background, Vadodara*
Left - Top
*The Dome of MS University - Faculty of Arts, Vadodara; this is the second largest dome in India*
Left - Bottom
*Main Durbar Hall, Laxmi Vilas Palace, Vadodara*

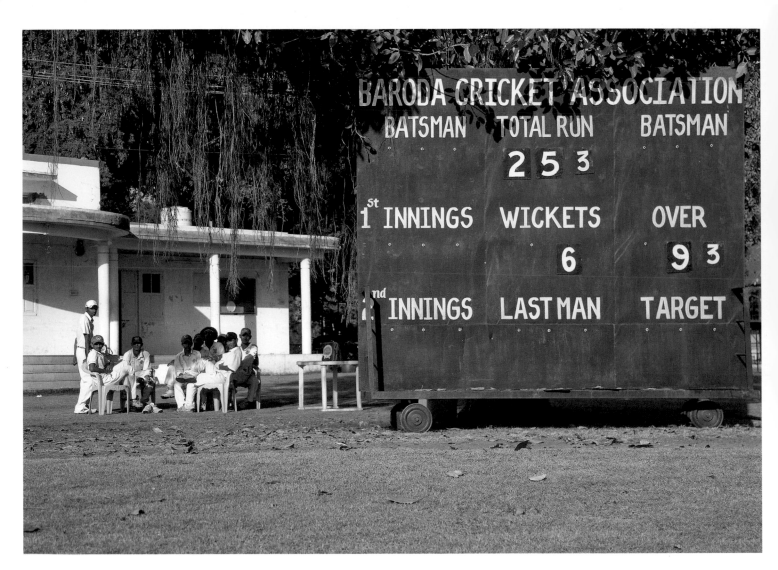

instructions about taking permission before travelling abroad. He even refused to follow protocol at King Edward's coronation.

Very much his own man, and very aware of the inevitable changes about to sweep through the subcontinent, he encouraged his officers of state to participate in the Congress sessions. He himself attended events organised by the Indian National Congress, including the 1906 Calcutta session.

He led by example, of course. One of the first things he did was to cut his own royal retinue from hundreds, down to a handful. At the same time, he launched radical reforms, completely overhauling the administration, and shifting magisterial responsibility from revenue officers to appointed judges. In 1902, he enacted a law to enable widow remarriage. In 1904, passed the Infant Marriage Prevention Act and Local Self-government Act, to devolve greater power to people.

Sayajirao had also launched a library movement. He set up at least 265 village libraries and 60 reading rooms. A well-travelled man, he sought inspiration for his reforms and education initiatives everywhere, looking both east and west.

Primary education was compulsory and free in his state. He first started schools in Amreli Mahal, one of the most backward areas, where children of both sexes and all castes were required to attend - an act that was nothing short of revolutionary in that age. Attendance was compulsory for girls between the age of seven and ten and for boys between the age of seven and twelve.

If local upper caste teachers refused to teach, he would employ Arya Samajis. He also opened up two hostels for 'untouchable' students and set up scholarships to help them to study further, including getting an education abroad. One of his beneficiaries was **BR Ambedkar**, to whom we owe, amongst other things, the Constitution of India.


Vadodara can also boast of a first class line-up in the field of the nation's primary passion, cricket. The city has the oldest cricket ground in Asia, Moti Baug, and another private cricket ground that hosts One Day International matches. It was a royal pastime and the former Indian cricketer and coach, Anshuman Gaekwad, was groomed in this city as was Datta Gaekwad, who was captain of the Indian team in 1959.

The Baroda Cricket Team has sent up several cricketers to the Indian A-list, including Vijay Hazare, Kiran More, Nayan Mongia, Anshuman Gaekwad, Ajay Jadeja and more recently Zaheer Khan, Irfan Pathan, Yusuf Pathan, and Jacob Martin.

Left - Top
*The historical Moti Baug Cricket grounds, Vadodara*

Left - Bottom
*Coaching the cricketers; Vadodara has produced some of the best Indian cricketers and is proud of its cricketing tradition in a country which practically venerates the sport*

Page 224-225
*Lalbhai Haveli, enroute from Gandhinagar to Ahmedabad; the original haveli was torn down piece-meal and re-constructed here in an endless and fabulously landscaped environment. A merchant who set up Arvind Mills, one of the largest suppliers of denim to the world, Lalbhai's five sons live with their families in havelis within this gated complex. You can see here the entrance, a sitting room and a view from a carved corner; what you cannot see are the ivory ceilings and other luxurious details*

# Bullish on Business

**When Gandhiji** started to mobilise people towards the ultimate goal of freedom from foreign rule, he was only drawing upon tradition. In Gujarat, people have always made common cause to protest – in their own interests and in the name of justice.

Gujarat has a very long history of collective action, at least in the larger cities such as Ahmedbad and Surat. Even in ancient times, there was a 'mahajan' for each trade – a sort of representative guild, while the town was headed by a *nagarsheth*, akin to a mayor. The city council had representatives of all occupational mahajans as well as some Patels who represented artisan communities. This council would fix rates of work, hours, holidays and so on and the nagarsheth could call for a strike. A complainant – anybody who felt that he/she had not been treated justly – had the right to go the mahajan seth's house and would neither drink water nor eat, nor move from the spot until the complaint was addressed.

When they acted in unison, the traders could bring the city to a standstill. On occasion, they did so too, quite simply by leaving the place. One of the instances in which the traders organised a collective action was in July 1616, when the officer of the Surat customs house assaulted a merchant. The whole community shut shop and left the city, refusing to return until the officer was dismissed.

Before that, there was a time when a local qazi was being unjust. The merchant class responded by leaving Surat; about eight thousand families left for Bharuch and from there, they sent a petition to the Mughal emperor Aurangzeb. This is one of the first recorded 'hartals' - strikes. It lasted about eight months and the traders won.

It is famously known in India that the language of Dalal Street (home to the Bombay Stock Exchange) is Gujarati. At least, it was so until the language of trading was officially established as English, in recent decades.

Dalal Street takes its name from Gujarati too; 'dalal' means broker and the first few brokers in Bombay were predominantly of Gujarati origin. Over the next century and a half, the stock market was practically ruled and run by a clutch of brokers and starting with the fabulously rich, if somewhat unscrupulous, broker Premchand Roychand in the nineteenth century, most of the brokers were Gujaratis. One testament to their continuing influence is that the Gujarati version of the BSE (Bombay Stock Exchange) website was launched before the Hindi version, although Hindi is the national language. Even now, some financial publications will insist on hiring candidates who are fluent in Gujarati.

"It all started under banyan trees and then a peepal tree, which stands till today. Around 1840, half a dozen brokers met under a banyan tree at the Town Hall, a few furlongs away from the present Dalal Street, where the imposing Jejeebhoy Towers that houses the Bombay Stock Exchange, reaches for the skies. By 1855, their numbers increased to 30-40 and they met under banyan trees... It was written at that time that "they were the privileged class that created a noise and obstructed traffic as they met on the street and the entrances of banks. Bank managers had to meander through their ranks to get to the upper floors. Everyone bowed to them and the police saluted them. In 1874, the brokers took

*Nature provides just enough and no more for our daily need. Hence it is also a theft to possess anything more than one's minimum requirement.*
Mohandas Karamchand Gandhi.

*The culture of commerce is very common here. Besides, Gujarat is almost fifty percent urbanised. This is unusual for any state and it reflects on our culture too. There were trade guilds even in ancient times, with an evolved dispute-settlement mechanism. There were mahajans and nagar-seths, like we have mayors for modern cities. The rural areas had developed their own systems. One group you'd find interesting is the Baharawatias. These were dacoits; literally meaning 'outlaw' in Gujarati. The strange thing was that each village had its own outlaw. The Baharwatia was held in very high regard, for he was responsible for keeping the village safe. The system of dacoity was completely enmeshed with the local social system.*

*Another fascinating community was the Bhats or Charans. They used to stand surety for others - loan takers, for example. They even stood surety for the Mughals and also served as bards for the rulers. Oh, they were a very colourful people! They'd cut their wrist if a promise (for which they had stood surety) was not kept, this was called 'tragu'. The community is considered sacred – 'devi-putra', they are called. Many generations of kings had given them grants of land. In fact, when the British tried to take away this land, there were major riots.*

**Arvind Shah**, sociologist.

Title inset
*Bharuch; Gujarat Gas CNG*
Left
*Jamnagar; The Reliance Petro-chemical refinery, the largest in the world*
Left - Bottom
*Mithapur; Tata Chemicals Limited*

premises near the present day Dalal Street, named after them, on a rent of Rs 130 per month and in 1895, they acquired a building for Rs 97,000 where there were two sturdy peepal trees."

[Extracted from an article by Olga Tellis, writing in the Asian Age, 2007]

If there's anybody who could lay claim to being a modern-day nawab from this state, it was **Dhirubhai Ambani**. He has, in fact, been described as the 'polyester prince'.

The man who was born Dhiralal Hirabhand Ambani, in Junagadh, incidentally belonged to the same community as Gandhiji – the Modh Banias. Ambani had started off as a dispatch clerk. When he was sent off to work in Aden, Yemen, he made himself a neat little package selling off Rials (Yemeni coin currency) as pure, melted silver, to the British. This was the first visible spark of his enterprise, which he himself later described as manipulation. He said, "I was a manipulator. A very good manipulator. I don't believe in not taking opportunities."

When he returned to India a decade later, there was scarcely an opportunity he did not take. It is common lore that he set up the Reliance group with just Rs 15,000. Starting with textiles, his company was soon one of the biggest names in the polyester fabric sector. 'Vimal' became one of the first few brands to be recognised throughout the country.

By the seventies, he was already offering equity to the people of Gujarat and they responded by the tens of thousands. There were so many shareholders that Reliance had to hold their annual general meetings in stadiums and *maidans* in Bombay. In the eighties, he successfully handled a bear cartel in the stock market that was trying to make Reliance share prices fall. It was a closely fought game, and though Reliance seemed to have the stomach for it, the Bombay Stock Exchange had to intervene. When the crisis had blown past, Ambani was even richer than before and the cynosure of all brokered eyes.

From textiles to petrochemicals to energy, power, telecommunications and retail – Reliance has continued to grow over the last five decades. It is one of the largest business groups in India, and at the time of Dhirubhai Ambani's death in 2002, the group had an annual turnover of at least Rs 75,000 crore or roughly US $ 12 billion. In recent years, the group has been divided between his two sons. **Mukesh Ambani** heads Reliance Industries Limited and **Anil Ambani** has taken over communication, capital and energy, under a different umbrella group, the Anil Dhirubhai Ambani Group.

*You do not require an invitation to make profits.*

**Dhirubhai Ambani**, entrepreneur

*His metier is the Ram-katha. But in his spare time he builds bridges across Hindu-Muslim 'borders' in Gujarat, advises the matriarch of India's top business family and raises Rs 20 crore for a cancer hospital in Vadodara.*

*But he doesn't think he's doing anything out of the ordinary. "Building bridges is my job as a Ram kathakar, that's what I am trying to do," Bapu says over the phone....*

*Later this week, the Ambani family is expected to meet Morari Bapu for advice and seek his blessings to resolve the squabble....*

*The 55-year-old is well-read in the scriptures and is highly regarded for his secular image. Besides Gujarat, he has a wide following among NRGs and NRIs in US, Canada, UK and Kenya. Born into a family of religious scholars in Talgajarda in Mahuva taluka in Bhavnagar district, 250 km from Ahmedabad, Morari Bapu took to 'Ram kathas' when he was 15. As he grew, so did his reputation for holding his audience spell-bound during his discourses....*

*A keen student and promoter of Gujarati literature, he has instituted the Narsinh Mehta Award which carries a Rs 1.51 lakh prize.*

[Extracted from an article by Janyala Sreenivas, in the Indian Express, Ahmedabad Newsline, 2004]

Left - 1
*Tata Salt and Chemicals, Mithapur, near Dwarka*
Left - 2
*Essar Petro-chemicals, Jamnagar*
Left - 3
*Solaris Chemical Plant, Kutch*
Left - 4
*Fertilizer Plant, Dahej*
Page 230 -231
*Malls and more malls. India's economic boom has created a retail environment where the local business is competing strongly with the big international brands*

# Sailing Forth

**Gujaratis living abroad** have always maintained strong ties with 'home'. They have helped causes dear to their own hearts in every way possible – through money, through political connections and social networks, through lobbying and forming associations and through investment in education and infrastructure.

Amongst the most significant ones who helped the freedom movement while living abroad, include names like **Bhikaiji Cama**, **Shyamji Krishna Varma**, **Sardarsinh Rana**. All three had lived overseas during the rise of Indian nationalism and aided the movement in their own way, whether it meant instituting scholarships to help bright youngsters study abroad, argue fiercely from public platforms, help shield revolutionaries or run arms.

In India, **Madame Cama** had even nursed the sick during the awful years of the plague. Unfortunately, she was forced to move abroad for health reasons and because of her involvement with the nationalist movement, she wasn't allowed to return home until 1935. She died soon after she returned.

Shyamji Varma, a disciple of **Swami Dayanand Saraswati** and an expert on Vedic philosophy and religion. When he eventually moved to London, his home was used as a base by many of the leaders of the freedom struggle. Sardarsinh Rana was rumoured to have helped smuggle arms for revolutionaries, while he lived in England and eventually, he did return to an Independent India. He died in Veraval.

In the nineteenth century, much of the money coming into Kutch arrived as money orders from expatriate Kutchis. They had gone to work abroad or to other cities in India. Part of the reason was that residents could not get permission to buy land outside the city limits. Under the last of the maharaos, the state bureaucracy was already a problem, especially for ambitious businessmen. In fact, when maharao Khengarji III was alive, money was short, so his son decided to sell off some royal land and develop housing colonies there. Though there were few takers locally, the colony was developed to the south – near Vaniawad – to cater to the rich Kutchi diaspora who wanted to retain property in Bhuj.

Even after the Jadeja administration came to end, on June 1st, 1948, the links with the diaspora remained strong. Members of the Kutchi Prajakiya Parishad had wanted to reinvest in Bhuj and also wanted to develop a traditional lifestyle, so they had asked the diaspora to reinvest in the city. That was how the new neighbouring township of Madhapar came about.

One of the Kutchi families who moved abroad in the nineteenth century included the Vassanjis. Their descendent is now a well-known author, **MG Vassanji**, who is the writer of books like The Gunny Sack, No New Land, Uhuru Street, Book of Secrets and most recently, The Assassin's Song.

Curiously, he started off working in the field of nuclear physics! But after the success of his first novel, he switched to writing full-time, and has since more than justified his career shift. He's won the Giller Prize, the Bressani Literary Prize and the Harbourfront Festival Prize, and now lives in Canada. As a young man, he read Dostoevsky, Conrad, and amongst his

*Top and Left*
*The ship-builders and their creations at Mandvi are descendants of the original dhow builders, dhows that plied the trade routes between Gujarat, Middle East, the East Coast of Africa - to Mozambique and Zanzibar. The ship-builders now build large modernised freight ships with wood from Indonesia, but they still use the old techniques and the ships are built entirely by hand and with wood. They sail now between India, the Middle East and Somalia*

influences, he counts Nehru and Gandhi. He picked, 'almost by accident', the autobiography of Nehru at a book sale, and it left an impact on him, and led him to read the autobiography of Mahatma Gandhi.

He points out that while most Gujaratis had gone to Africa as shopkeepers (in the nineteenth century), Gujarat has had a much longer association with East Africa, for trade ties had existed for millenia. Even Vasco da Gama had landed at Calicut only with the help and guidance of two Gujaratis whom he had picked up en route, in Mombasa.

Vassanji was born in Kenya and grew up in Tanzania. His mother's mother was from Jam Jodhpur, near Jamnagar, and his mother's father was from Porbandar. His father's grandfather came from Una, near Junagadh. Not surprisingly, he's been described as Indian-African-Canadian.

Ask him where, in the midst of all this, is the 'Gujarati', and he tells you that "Gujarati – a part of Gujarati, which is diverse – was almost an instinctual part of my growing up. I grew up speaking Gujarati and Kutchi; my children speak some Kutchi. We played the *daandiya* and *raas* (*garba*) at festivals, which were major events in our lives; and the *ginans* that we sang daily in our *khano* (prayer house) were in older forms of Gujarati and Sindhi. I must also mention our foods: the snacks – *chevda*, *gaathia*, *dhokra*, *churma na laddoo*, etc, also two types of *khichdi*, *bajra rotla*, *lassan na laddoo* (are) always associated with *desh*."

While being uprooted is never easy, his family went through it twice, as did many others who followed that particular route to the west. He describes the process of relocating as a sort of evolution.

"Among my people, the Khojas, they simply went on evolving. We had looked to Britain more than India – like good colonials – anyway. But we still speak Kutchi or Gujarati and, I believe, forms of the *daandiya* and *raas* are played by the young; and among many, the *ginans* are still loved. There is a recognition of India and Gujarat as the ancestral place and people often visit."

In the meantime, his memories include distant, half-remembered stories in relation to the land of his ancestors. "I remember mythical stories – a pir arriving a very long time ago and playing the *raas* for a group of villagers. Stories of mythological rajas and ranis, related in a religious-mystical way. And a story my grandmother told us of how she and her sister got lost one day while going to fetch water. Unfortunately, the colonial influence was profound, and I was too young to ask about other things. There is another story of my father stowing away on a ship bound for Bombay and not being allowed to disembark because he did not have papers or money. Then, there was an uncle who landed in Bombay and immediately came back, depressed by the poor people he saw.

However, he does not believe that the expat community is any more traditional than families in urban India, or that they hold tighter to cultural practices from another age. He tells you, "Our women gave up the *pachedi* (the practice of covering the head) in the 1940s; all the girls finished school; the language evolved, so that Swahili words were often used in place of the Gujarati (for example, for 'bowl' and 'orange'). Many of the kumbhad caste became mechanics. Marriage restrictions (between Kutchis and Kathiawadis) disappeared and so on... There would always be new immigrants, of course, who would stick to the old ways."

Top
*The tented resort at Sham-e-Sharad, Hodka, Kutch*
Left
*Fishing boat at Bet Dwarka*

# Another City By the Sea

**Bhavnagar**. As the name suggests, the city was founded in 1723 by **Bhavsinhji Gohil**, as the capital of his new kingdom. The Gohil Rajputs in Marwar (Rajasthan) had been having a hard time in their own region and they decided to move south, in the thirteenth century. Initially, they established three capitals – Sejakpur, Umrala and Sihor. The region was sometimes also called 'Gohilwad'.

When Sihor was attacked by Khanthaji Kadani and Pilaji Gaekwad, the then-ruler Bhanvsinhji Gohil realised that his capital was very vulnerable and decided to relocate to Vadva village, which he renamed after himself: Bhavnagar.

It was a good location since it had the potential of sea trade, then a major source of revenue. Bhavsinhji was a cautious ruler who realised the importance of protecting revenues sources. He immediately entered into agreements with the Siddis of Janjira who used to control the Castle of Surat, giving them a share of the taxes, and after the British took over Surat, he forged similar agreements with them. He also developed other ports like Mahuva and Gogha.

As Bhavnagar prospered, the rulers began to make moves towards modernisation. Bhavsinji got railways built in the state in the eighteenth century. His grandson Vakhatsinhji Gohil began to expand the territory after taking over land that belonged to the Kolis and the Kathis.

The last ruler, Sir Krishnakumar Sinhji handed over his kingdom to Sardar Patel in 1948; it became the first princely state to join the union of India.

Now the fifth-largest city in Gujarat, Bhavnagar is also known as the cultural capital of Saurashtra. It is known for having given Gujarat many famous writers such as Jhaverchand Meghani, Kavi Kant and Dula Kag. Narsinh Mehta too was born in Talaja, a village that is now in Bhavnagar district.

It is believed that **Narsinh Mehta** was born in Talaja village into a Nagar Brahmin family in the early fifteenth century. After his mother died, he married Manekbai.

Narsinh and his wife went to live with his cousin Bansidhar, in Junagadh. According to legend, his *bhabhi*, his brother's wife, was always taunting and insulting Narsinh. When he couldn't take it any more, he left the house and went to a forest to fast and meditate. After seven days, Lord Shiva appeared. Narsinh wanted to see Vrindavan, for he was a great devotee of Krishna. Lord Shiva took him to Vrindavan where he witnessed the eternal *raas leela* – the divine dance – of Krishna with the gopis. After this, a transformed Narsinh went back home, touched his *bhabhi's* feet and thanked her for all the insults.

He continued to live in Junagadh with his wife and two children. Through the rest of his life, he mixed with *sadhus* and *bhakts* – saints and

Title inset
*Bhavnagar; silhouette of a monument*
Left
*Bhavnagar; an evening chat sitting against a beautiful heritage*

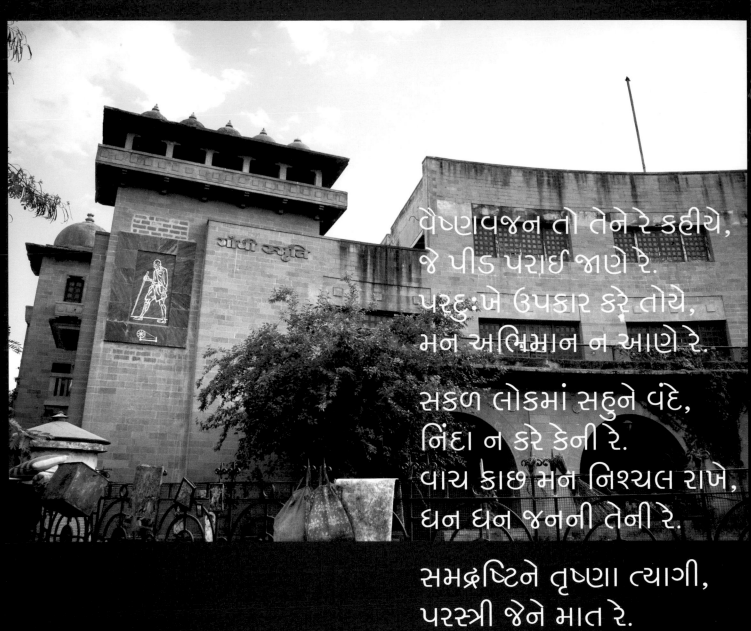

વૈષ્ણવજન તો તેને રે કહીયે,
જે પીડ પરાઈ જાણે રે.
પરદુઃખે ઉપકાર કરે તોયે,
મન અભિમાન ન આણે રે.

સકળ લોકમાં સહુને વંદે,
નિંદા ન કરે કેની રે.
વાચ કાછ મન નિશ્ચલ રાખે,
ધન ધન જનની તેની રે.

સમદ્રષ્ટિને તૃષ્ણા ત્યાગી,
પરસ્ત્રી જેને માત રે.
જિહ્વા થકી અસત્ય ન બોલે,
પરધન નવ ઝાલે હાથ રે.

મોહ માયા વ્યાપે નહિ જેને,
દ્રઢ વૈરાગ્ય જેના મનમાં રે.
રામ નામ શું તાળી રે વાગી,
સકળ તિરથ તેના તનમાં રે.

વણલોભી ને કપટ રહિત છે,
કામ ક્રોધ નિવાર્યા રે.
ભણે નરસૈયો તેનું દર્શન કરતા,
કુળ ઈકોતેર તાર્યા રે.

devotees – and all whom he considered 'Hari's subjects', subjects of the Lord, or Harijans. He also acquired a bad reputation for he would sing and dance with women, who were also followers of Krishna. Often insulted and always poor, Narsinh went on singing about Krishna and the eternal *raas*.

Narsinh's works can no longer be found in the original. They were transmitted orally for the most part and the work underwent changes of text, accent and form as it was passed from one group to the other.

One of Mahatma Gandhi's favourite bhajans is also attributed to Narsinh Mehta, where he describes what a true 'Vaishnav' life is like.

*He is the true Vaishnava who knows
and feels another's woes as his own*

*Ever ready to serve others who
are unhappy, he never lets
vanity get to his head*

*Bowing to everyone humbly
and criticising none*

*He keeps his speech, deeds and
thoughts pure; blessed is the
mother who begets such a one*

*He looks upon all with an equal eye.
Having rid himself of lust, he treats and
reveres every woman as his mother*

*His tongue would fail him if he
attempted to utter an untruth. He
does not covet another's wealth*

*The bonds of earthly attachment
hold him not. His mind is deeply
rooted in renunciation*

*Every moment he is intent on reciting
the name of the Lord Rama. All the
holy places are ever present in his body*

*He has conquered greed, deceit,
passion (lust) and anger*

*The sight of such a Vaishnava, says
Narsinh, saves a family through
seventy-one generations*

# Utterly, Butterly Doable

**Amul** (Anand Milk-producers Union Limited) is the frontispiece of the dairy co-operative movement in the country, and though it started in Gujarat, the model has been replicated in many other states, under different brand names.

Amul is owned by about 2.6 million milk producers in Gujarat, and Anand is known as the town that saw this incredible feat accomplished.

Lying mid-way between Ahmedabad and Vadodara, the town is known as the milk capital and the centre of the 'white revolution' in India, a process of upping milk production and diversifying into various dairy products so that India eventually became the largest producer of milk in the world.

The rest, as they say, is history.

There is a lot of history associated with Amul, come to think of it. The success of the co-operative dairy model caused Operation Flood, or the 'white revolution', which marked wide-spread access to milk in India. Dairy farming became a profitable business.

The story of Amul led to the making of 'Manthan', probably the only film in the history of cinema that has been funded by 500,000 doodh-wale (milk-men/maids).

Another bit of history is lodged in Amul Butter's advertising campaign, which may well be the longest running campaign with the same theme. Anybody who has grown up in Indian cities is familiar with hoardings or print ads with the popular rounded mascot making witty, irreverent remarks about whoever or whatever is the news of the moment. Utterly, Butterly Delicious!

(If you love and miss those hoardings, check out http://www.amul.com/hits.html. The whole archive is available!)

Until Amul came along, though, there was only Polson. Farmers had to travel long distances and since milk was a very perishable commodity, they were forced to sell it at whatever price was being offered. There was little technology available locally, for storing or modifying milk, and they had no access to fair marketing.

That's when the freedom fighter-activist **Tribhovandas Patel** decided to organise farmers, starting with Kheda, the district Sardar Patel belonged to and which had been the starting point for one of the most significant anti-imperial protests before independence. Anand was a part of this district at that time. In 1946, the Anand Milk-producers Union Limited was formed. AMUL, which in Hindi means 'priceless'.

In 1948, there were only 400 farmers who were part of this diary movement. Today, there are millions.

Six decades later, Amul can well lay claim to being the 'taste of India'. It has given us much more than milk. There is butter, cheese, spreads, ghee, curds, chocolate, shrikhand, paneer, packaged sweets, flavoured milk drinks, butter-milk, whipped cream... and each year, there's something new being offered by the brand.

*Ideas are no one's monopoly*
**Dhirubhai Ambani**, entrepreneur

*In our time, all you saw was Polson butter. Then, suddenly, Amul happened. Tribhuvandas Patel was instrumental in organising the farmers and cattle-owners in Anand on a co-operative basis. He set up the first few milk co-operatives and then, the rest...*
**Arvind Shah**, sociologist

Title inset
*Marked milk-cans; Anand*

Top 1
*Utterly, butterly, delicious - Amul*

Top 2
*The gleaming milk silos at the Amul Milk plant, which is totally computerised and practically untouched by human hands*

Left - Top
*Anand; Village collection centres where the villagers bring in milk every morning; it is checked for fat content and they are paid accordingly*

Left - Bottom
*Buffaloes at a 'gaoshala', with an egret for company; Anand*

Top
*...and the women return home as well*

Left
*Returning home at the end of the day's*
*journey; a tribal with his cattle*

243

# What Lies Beyond

'He was sometimes called the Gardener, because he loved gardens, and he tended his followers like seedlings. He had yet another, curious name, Kaatil, or Killer, which thrilled us children no end. But its provenance was less exciting: he had a piercing look, it was said, sharp as an arrow, and an intellect keen as the blade of a rapier, using which he won many debates in the great courts of the kings. "Look, Karsan," said Bapu-ji. He pointed out the bright planets overhead, the speckle that was the North Star, at the constellations connected tenuously by their invisible threads. "When I was young," he said, "I wished only to study the stars... But that was a long time ago, and a different world...

"But what lies above the stars?" he asked, after the pause, his voice rising a bare nuance above my head. "That is the important question I had to learn. What lies beyond the sky? What do you see when you remove this dark speckled blanket covering our heads?

Nothing? But what is nothing?"'

from The Assassin's Song (author **M G Vassanji**), Penguin India

*Title inset*
*...a modern new Gujarat - the Ahmedabad - Vadodara expressway*

*Top*
*A patriotic Indian Gujarat, as the kites quite rightly tell you*

*Left*
*On the fast track to a new, young Gujarat*

# Reference

## Books

Bhuj: Art, Architecture, History, Azhar Tyabji, Mapin Publishing, Ahmedabad, 2006

Contemporary Art in Baroda, Gulam Muhammed Sheikh, Tulika Books, 1997

The Assassin's Song, M G Vassanji, Viking Penguin Books India, 2007

The Shaping of Modern Gujarat: Plurality, Hindutva and Beyond, Achyut Yagnik and Suchitra Sheth, Penguin India, New Delhi, 2005

## Poetry

Celebration of Divinity, a collection of Bhakti poems by Narsinh Mehta; Translated by Darshana Trivedi and Rupalee Burke; Gujarati Sahitya Akademi 2001

Gayatri, Coral Island, a collection of poetry by Niranjan Bhagat; Translated by Suguna Ramanathan and Rita Kothari; Gujarati Sahitya Akademi 2003

Patro, Coral Island, a collection of poetry by Niranjan Bhagat; Translated by Suguna Ramanathan and Rita Kothari; Gujarati Sahitya Akademi 2003

Salagri Havao, Samvedan Sanskritic Manch, Ahmedabad 1995

Wali Muhammad Wali; Translated by Aakar Patel

Wali Muhammad Wali; Translation by Sunil Sharma; from Kulliyat-e Vali, edited by Nur al-Hasan Hashmi

## Newspapers and Magazines

Indian Express

The Asian Age

The Tribune

Times of India

## Websites

http://en.wikipedia.org/wiki/Jai_Jai_Garavi_Gujarat

http://en.wikipedia.org/wiki/Vaishnav_jan_to

http://www.rajendrashukla.com/Archives0002.html

http://www.readgujarati.com/sahitya/?p=346

www.amul.com

www.bhasharesearch.org

## Others

On a gravestone: Catherine Theresa Allen, 31st Dec, 1857

Left
*Traditional decorated storage
container made of clay*

# Index

# Photographer's Note

**"You don't take a photograph, you ask, quietly, to borrow it."**

Anon

Over 4000 kilometers, traversing the Rann of Katchh, the princely states of Kathiawar, the verdant bamboo forests of the Dangs and pristine shorelines of Saurashtra, Gujarat opened her doors to me. I moved amongst her people akin to a traveller many centuries ago, moving with the wind into the open doors of havelis and palaces.

Photographing this journey took me to some of the remotest parts of India. The unforgiving Great Rann, became hotter as the days went by. The summer winds blowing across the vast barren flatlands would reach over 50 degrees by mid June. Little survives here. On the horizon I saw the Jat nomads with their camel trains glide effortlessly over the salt flats in search of pastures for their camels and goats. Their hardy lives are a testament to their adaptability in this hostile environment. My passage continued south, to the lush Narmada Valley, where sugarcane and cotton fields stretched beyond the limits of sight; the massive canals transport life-giving water to arid region and turning the countryside into shades of green. In the west the Asiatic lions of the Gir stalked the forest floor as the golden sun set behind giant Sal trees. In the Princely states of Baroda and Vansda the royals turn their attention away from hunting to the conservation of the flora and fauna by setting up protected sanctuaries.

Everywhere I went people opened their doors to me. As a photographer one attracts curious onlookers always ready to lend a helping hand or tell you a tale that the guidebooks won't. From fables, to folklore, poetry to *shers*, Gujarat's many stories are shared by her people. Men such as Shabbir Malik, the great old man of the Rann, whose passion extends beyond wildlife conservation to the protection of the very fabric of the tribes that bind the Rann together. Or Dr. Ayaz Khan, who stoically has given his entire life to education and continues today to open the minds of Gujarat's children. These are the unsung heroes of Gujarat, people who make this great state what she is. I met many of them on this journey, and their perspectives colour the story of my images. It is also in this corner of the world that I grew to be thankful for new and lasting friendships.

As a photographer it is the colours of Gujarat that have been my muse. The stark beauty of her land and the rich textures of her textiles, the azure waters of the miles of coastline and the gastronomic vividness of her food have guided my eye and my lens.

My hope is that this visual journey brings justice to this great state, her ancient history and her drive to the forefront of modern India.

Karam K. Puri
New Delhi 2008

## Acknowledgements

The photographs in this book would not have been possible without the generosity of the people of Gujarat. I would particularly like to thank Mr. Ravi Singh, Lt. Gen. Rostum Nanavatty, Veer Nanavatty, Kanika Puri, Karma Vir Singh of Jambughora, Samarjit Gaekwad of Baroda, H.H. Digvirendra Singh Solanki of Vansda, Mr. Shabbir Malik, Dhanraj Malik, Mike Vaghella, Parinjay Singhji of Mandvi, Mr. Jahangir Vakil, Dr. Ayaz Khan, Nitesh Kotechar, Ranjit Singh Parmar, Mr. Jai-Inder Singh, Jayshree Lalbhai, Tarun, SV Photographic and Ezara.

Parting from Gujarat leaves thorns in my chest
My heart – on fire! – pounds impatiently in my breast
What cure can heal the wound of living apart?
The scimitar of exile has cut deep into my heart
My feet were bound, and in sorrow I did tire
My heart singed rapidly, like a hair over fire
At first, this heady stroll left my mind fertile with rumination
In the end, this separation pulled my heart into intoxication
Gaze into my heart and see the garden of the lover
Where the flowers of winter riot in my blood's colour
It is with regret that in the end I see my friends depart
So rise from the empty tavern and steady yourself, my heart
And thank God's mercy, O Wali! He let that passion remain
The heart's still anxious to catch a glimpse of my Gujarat again.

# Dar Firaaq-e-Gujarat
## (On Parting From Gujarat)

**Wali Muhammad Wali** (1667-1707),
also known as Wali Gujarati.
(Translated by Aakar Patel.)